THE SERVICE OF A PARSON

THE SERVICE
OF A PARSON

Why he is there—and what he does

by

EDWARD CARPENTER
Archdeacon of Westminster

Sponsored by the
Central Advisory Council for the Ministry

HODDER AND STOUGHTON

Copyright © 1965 by the
Central Advisory Council for the Ministry

First printed 1965

PRINTED AND BOUND IN GREAT BRITAIN FOR
HODDER AND STOUGHTON LIMITED, ST. PAUL'S
HOUSE, WARWICK LANE, LONDON, E.C.4 BY
C. TINLING AND CO. LIMITED, LIVERPOOL,
LONDON AND PRESCOT

Dedicated with gratitude and affection to:
My father and mother, who introduced me into the
life of the Church of England
Arthur Cuming, my first vicar
George Saywell, my rector when ordained
Also to the parishioners of Stanmore

CONTENTS

FOREWORD

By the BISHOP OF LINCOLN (Chairman of the
Central Advisory Council for the Ministry
of the Church of England)

THIS book has been written by Archdeacon Edward Carpenter at the request of the Central Advisory Council for the Ministry. He was asked to write the book in his own way; C.A.C.T.M. welcomes and gladly sponsors his work, though not necessarily sharing his viewpoint in every detail. The book is opportune because of the author's deep and enthusiastic conviction about the relevance and importance of the parochial ministry at the present time. The Paul Report is in itself a great vindication of the parochial ideal of the Church of England, but the careful appraisal in that report of the present situation of the parochial ministry may have caused doubts of the essential place of parochial clergy in the national life. I believe that this book shows most clearly the great and unique opportunities which confront the ordained minister of the church at the present time. It is the recognition of these great opportunities which should restore confidence, prompt such reforms as are needed, and evoke new vocations to the historic ministry of the Church of England.

KENNETH LINCOLN

CHAPTER I

AN INHERITANCE

THE following book about the clergy of the Church of England is, in the main, concerned with those who live and work in an English parish. This is a right perspective, for out of the 15,754 ordained ministers active in this country at the present time, some 13,438 are employed in this way.* It is natural, therefore, that when the average Englishman thinks of a parson, it is usually of the man who takes weddings, baptises babies, and officiates at funerals.

There are, of course, many other kinds of clergymen undertaking a variety of responsibilities, but it is the local man, living near his own church and amongst his own people, who may be taken as most typical and representative. In a sense he is in the front line. Certainly he is one of the most familiar ingredients in the English scene, and he is so because he has been with it for a long time, in fact for well over a thousand years. Indeed, his story begins when the marauding, Teutonic tribes settled in England way back in the fifth century A.D. bringing with them their primitive religion. Unlike the Romano-British people whom they drove to the west, these German invaders preferred the open countryside to the strategically planned towns of a more advanced civilisation. They consequently settled in small village communities, so that when they became Christians in the years following Augustine's Roman mission of A.D. 597, it was natural for the pagan priest to become the Christian minister. Scarcely distinguishable in economic standing from the meanest villager around him, and usually

* Some 1,223 clergymen, ordained in the Church of England, are at present working overseas. There are also, of course, a large number of parsons of the Anglican communion who were ordained outside England, over 340 in Scotland, about 1,100 in Wales, and many more in other lands.

both appointed and maintained by the local lord, his religious functions in the new Faith set him apart, and gave him a unique status. In spite of the passing of centuries, and the changes which such passage of time has brought about to his place within society, his real task has remained very much the same, though he may set about it in far different ways. Essentially he is a minister of the Christian church, a church which exists for one purpose, and one purpose only, namely to give glory to God by witnessing to and building His Kingdom through commitment to Jesus.

How precisely he is to do this, and what it means in the present technological age, will I hope become clearer as this book proceeds. My primary concern in what follows will not be with past history, interesting though this history is, but with the exigencies and challenges of the 1960's. Nostalgia for what has been can become dangerous when it leads to an escape from the realities of the present; the more so as the past is all too often allowed to bask in the reflected aura of an after-glow. Yet it is essential, if we wish to understand the parish priest of to-day, and be sensitive both to the sort of man that he is and the work that he is doing, to know something of the inheritance into which he has entered, if only to recognise how vastly changed his present estate is. Yet the thousand years of a history in which he has been intimately involved cannot be entirely blotted out in the twinkling of an eye, particularly when that history is interwoven with the developing life of a great nation— a nation, moreover, upon which Christian Faith has brought to bear, in intention at least, a transcendental dimension. This is the more significant because this Faith is not world renouncing but world affirming. It believes that God is working a purpose out in history as year succeeds to year, and that the incarnation of Christ in time leads necessarily here and now to the building of a city that has firm foundations. In other words, and more simply, that the well-being of society is of concern to God as it must be to man.

The English parish priest of the mid-twentieth century has entered into a many-sided inheritance, such that he cannot easily forswear and which for better or for worse still affects his day-to-day life. It still has a conditioning influence on other people's reactions to him. This inheritance may be briefly summarised.

First, as a priest he is a minister of holy things. On Sundays, at least, he leads his people in worship (or some of them!), and at the significant moments of human life—birth, marriage and death—he engages in religious acts which relate these elemental experiences to God's will and purpose. This continuing and day-to-day ministry across the centuries has given to him a specialised status and has made ordinary people regard him in a unique way. He has stood, often in spite of himself, for the awesomeness and mystery of things, for the passing and ephemeral nature of human affairs, for the fact that here men have no abiding city. His very presence in the parish has been evocative of, or at least associated with, a range of experience into which men do as a matter of fact enter, explain this experience how they will. He stands for the sacred. His functions as a priest, and his worshipful character generally, have spoken to certain elemental depths in the most utilitarian of men. In this respect he is a representative person, expressing something other than and beyond himself. Indeed, if he did not exist, it may be that society would have to invent him in another form, in the same way as the French philosopher, Comte, required priests for his religion of humanity. Even such an essentially secular figure as Parson Woodforde, in the eighteenth century, could not entirely escape from the fact that he had to discharge a particular function in his church and that this made him, in the eyes of his villagers, a different sort of person. It does not follow that modern technological man has transcended this need.

Secondly, the parish priest enters into a specifically Christian inheritance. He is, as we say, a minister of the word and sacrament. He mediates a Faith, built upon a truth of existence, and embodied in a way of life. He stands for an order of persons and for a community arising out of particular historic events associated with Jesus. He is not simply a private person seeking to do good: but a commissioned agent witnessing to specific truths about God and man, the latter made meaningful within a visible society.

Thirdly, the parish priest has behind him a past which is, and in the nature of the case must be, peculiar to the English scene, namely the past of a semi-governmental official and, in the middle of the nineteenth century, of a country gentleman. A little history will be necessary to illustrate this aspect of his mixed personality.

When the Teutonic tribes came over to England from their native Germany, they found that they could not take up the old life, where they had left it, in a new country. They now needed support in a mood of uncertainty, a Faith more adequate to their changed situation. The Christian Gospel came to them with the prestige of Roman civilisation and the consequence was that the English nation, to use the expressive words of the historian, J. R. Green, grew up as 'the child of the church'. This church provided the only civil service that the country was to know for centuries. It gave a vision of unity, while the nation was still divided: it sanctified kingship, and engendered respect for the law as an expression of the divine will. The parish priest, in the locality, played a significant rôle in this civilising mission; and after the Reformation, when gradually his social and economic status rose, he began to assume even greater importance, especially in small village communities. Under the Elizabethan legislation, he (with his churchwardens) was charged with many responsibilities in connection with what we should now call local government. The nineteenth century, if it took away some of these legal powers, added to them in other ways. The Victorian era was a time of progress and expansion, and the parish priest was able to exert an enormous influence on the social life of his village. Often a younger son of the squire, a large employer of labour, chairman of the local board of school managers—he probably founded the school—also, maybe, a justice of the peace, he possessed a unique opportunity of giving direction and exercising authority. In his hands were entrusted many local charities, and this at a time when social services as we know them were yet unborn, and a few shillings could make all the difference between a tolerable existence and utter penury, with the workhouse round the corner. Seldom has so much potential local authority been concentrated in the hands of one man, for in him the mana of the priest, and the status of a Christian clerk in holy orders, were joined with the prestige of a country gentleman. He was indeed thoroughly integrated into the contemporary class structure and as a result felt secure and at home in it. He moved easily and on terms of equality with his more aristocratic neighbours; he was usually a man of great personal independence—as well as of independent means —and his vicarage, with its abundant supply of cheap domestic labour and innumerable children, hummed with activity. The annual garden party held on its spacious lawn was a village event and the whole gamut of 'penny readings', magic lantern shows, thrift clubs, choir festivals, village concerts, Sunday-school outings, were usually organised from the parsonage house. Such church-sponsored activity, unknown in the eighteenth century when it would have been considered unnecessary, was paradoxically an indication that the village, as a self-contained social and economic unit, was already breaking up. A division was developing between church and parish, with the consequence that if the former were to continue to direct the life of the latter, it would have to do something about it. The parson must exert leadership, be active, recreate the integrity of the local community by making the church a focal point for its unity. In this endeavour he was fortunate, for being a country gentleman still counted for much, and there was as yet no welfare state, no insurance or health schemes, no clubs run by the local authority. The opportunities for initiative were thus boundless. It was by and large—there were exceptions of course —a great time for the country parson.

The city presented a different problem and often a more difficult one, though England was still, until late in the nineteenth century, largely a rural society. The market town and the wealthy suburbs were, it is true, easily contained within the parochial system: but to the classes recruited by the Industrial Revolution, the Church of England seemed largely allied with the enemy, and was rejected accordingly. In the main, such large centres of population were untouched by the church, though even here there emerged the slum priest, making his church a centre for relief, and creating a community of the dispossessed around it.

Fourthly, the parish priest enters into an inheritance which is of a more professional character, and which dates from the last century. Consideration of this, however, will be left to the next chapter.

Enough has perhaps now been said to illustrate that the parish priest of to-day has behind him a past in which priesthood has become blended with social and even political responsibilities. It is important to remember this, for no-one can begin to understand the 'job' of an Anglican parson to-day, and its difficulties in the present, unless he knows something of the more than religious history which has brought him to the place where he is. True it is, of course, that the social scene which I have sketched above, though in certain aspects it is not more than a hundred years old, seems to us now as dead as the Dodo, indeed almost as if it had never been. Yet the parish priest cannot be entirely unaffected by this vanished splendour. Every day—at least for many a parson—his large house and (maybe) ill-kept garden remind him of a former greatness. Nor do long accustomed attitudes to an office disappear so completely as to leave not a rack behind. They can persist, with diminished intensity, to embarrass the present and to hinder the emergence of a more relevant pattern. They may, however, still represent a potential source of strength if rightly drawn upon. Every vagrant with his hard luck story who knocks on the vicarage door is bearing witness to a tradition which goes back a thousand years. Whatever the Established Church has set out to do in the seats of power at the centre has for centuries been implemented (or not) by the professional representative on the spot, the parish priest. He has been the instrument, sometimes an unwilling one, by which political pressures, moral purges, and religions revolutions have been introduced into the life and consciousness of the local community. True he works under the general superintendence of his diocesan bishop who is a figure in national affairs; and he exists alongside other kinds of clergymen—university dons, deans, canons, chaplains, to mention but a few. Yet the burden of trying to make England a Christian country has fallen heavily upon him, labouring in season and out of season where he lives, in his parish. And the parish itself arose not primarily as a religious but as a social and economic unit.

At its best, the inheritance of the parish priest is one of involvement in the national life with no clear-cut distinction between the sacred and the secular. His story is part of the history of a church, which in building the Kingdom, has dared to dirty its hands.

CHAPTER 2

PREPARATION

(1) VOCATION

THERE are in England some 14,491 parishes served by 13,438 clergymen. Why are these men there, and how, or by what process, was this brought about?

The immediate answer is the rather Irish one, namely that they are there because they are priests of the Church of England, and this is what they believe they ought to be. On the human side, the whole process begins from within the man himself. No one becomes a clergyman, or ought not to anyhow, unless he feels some kind of inner compulsion, some general sense that this is his vocation. When he is commissioned or set apart for this work and status by the bishop on behalf of the church as a whole, he is asked: 'Do you think in your heart you (are) truly called?' It is only on a frank but humble reply, 'I think it,' that the ordination goes forward.

This consciousness of being called, of experiencing a vocation, need not be something agonising or dramatic, though in some men it is. More often it stems from a general sense of duty; from a sustained conviction that this is the work that a man ought to be doing; that this is for him; that here is a challenging and worth-while job to be done. For example, I remember a man in his late fifties, a journalist, who came to feel that he must offer himself for the priesthood. He put it this way: 'If the church authorities think that I am not suitable, I shall accept their judgment and rest content: but I shall not rest content until I have made the offer. I am sure I must do this.'

A vocation felt in this way by the older and more mature usually comes from a growing experience of men and affairs; not from disgust with the world and writing it off in despair, but rather from glimpsing the vast possibilities of living, yet the need, if man is to fulfil himself, of both vision and power. In the young a sense of vocation often arises, and properly, from an enthusiastic idealism which is concerned to put the world right.

However brought about, recruitment into the ranks of the clergy rests upon an essentially free act. If the call comes from without through the Spirit of God which 'bloweth where it listeth', this call is experienced as an inward constraint. I believe that a possible ordinand should not be too precious, that is too curious, in respect of the motives leading to ordination. Excessive introspection in a matter of this kind often leads to morbidity, to lack of confidence, to ineffectiveness and to the doubt which saps the mind. Pure motives are a figment of the Puritan imagination. A genuine call may often consist simply in a lively feeling that here is a worth-while calling which offers a vast possibility of service to one's fellow men—and that I ought seriously to consider whether it is for me. Some of the best clergymen have been led to ordination in a seemingly pedestrian and unexciting way. Usually such men have subsequently shown a determined willingness to work hard, a refusal to be easily disappointed, and a robust commonsense, all of which have proved invaluable. A too romantic or pietistic view of what a call to the priesthood implies can all too easily end in frustration and a sense of failure. One of the most conscientious of English clergymen, Edmund Gibson, Bishop of London, sought ordination only after being somewhat disillusioned with his prospects at the bar. Yet his devotion to the cause of Christ proved to be lifelong.

Certainly a dedication of this kind, rooted in a somewhat uncomplicated response to what is thought to be a duty, often lies behind the simple affirmation: 'I think it.'

In some men, of course, the call to the priesthood *is* of a more critical, even dramatic character, such as to take them away from their present work and almost against their will drive them into this other 'estate'. The activity of the Spirit cannot be confined within our preconceived notions as to how or where He ought to operate, though He can be impeded in his constraining work by self-will or lack of sensitivity to his promptings.

A clergyman, then, must entertain a sense of being called, by which is meant that basically he must experience an inner constraint prompting him to undertake this responsibility, to be this kind of person. This sense of *oughtness* or obligation can assume many forms, and both the nature of the compulsion and the manner in which it is conveyed or apprehended (i.e. happens) will vary from person to person. In some people the call is so clear and strong as to be unequivocal. Only one response to it is morally possible. In others it is more cloudy and obscure, so much so that at times they may well doubt its reality. The call may have come to them, as we say, like a bolt from the blue, perhaps by someone suggesting: 'Do you think you ought to be ordained?'—and the question stuck. Or it may have originated in a simple desire to do good.

Such reflections lead to the question: What kind of person does the Church need for its ordained ministry? The answer can only be that it needs many kinds. The priesthood requires its prophets, though not everybody is called upon to be one, and Heaven defend us from the self-appointed seer, who mistakes the fog of ignorance for penetration into the cloudy mystery of the Shekinah of God. When the prophet does arise he will inevitably give fervent utterance to his outpourings come what may. The priestly vocation might even shackle him, though it is essential that some priests should also be prophets. The priesthood also needs its rebels, but it cannot exist solely on these, though there is little danger, I fear, that so abundant a supply will ever be forthcoming. By and large the priest in the parish must be more patient, more tolerant, more understanding than the prophet or rebel is inclined to be. He must take people as they are, with their prejudices and timidity, and wean them out of such short-comings, here a little there a little.

The fact is that many different kinds of persons are needed, different in temperament, in age, in the nature of their gifts, in social and educational background. The Anglican priest must not be made to measure, nor cut to one uniform pattern. He must not become a type.

For ordination to the priesthood a man must have reached twenty-four years of age, be baptised, and a confirmed member of the Church of England. This means that he must be fully engrafted into a branch of that continuing community which the life, death and resurrection of Jesus brought to birth, and which, so Christians believe, His Spirit still energises. Here again we see a distinction between the priest and the prophet. In respect of the latter, the Deity obviously makes no such requirement.

Such baptism need not be of long standing, for it would be quite wrong and inappropriate to confine entry into the ministry to those who have been introduced into membership of the Church of England as children, and who have lived and asserted such membership across the years. Many ordinands do, of course, come from Christian homes, and it is right that a parish priest should seek to foster vocations in his own congregation. But some men need the ripened experience of living, even of estrangement, and the challenge which comes to them through involvement in the affairs of the world, to be led into a conscious Christ commitment. What the requirement of baptism and confirmation is meant to secure is that the potential priest is himself a dedicated member of the community in which he is to exercise his particular ministry. Such membership may be short or long, measured in length of years. What matters is its quality, its range, its depth and maturity. Doubtless in the case of some people it is their call and desire to give their lives to Christ through the priesthood which leads to baptism and confirmation. A man may be called first, and only later introduced to Christian Faith, as in a measure happened to St. Paul. The Spirit does not restrict his activities to the comprehension of formal minds, nor adjust his pressures to conform with the laws of churches. It may at first seem odd that Jacob was preferred to Esau. A society which has at its heart loyalty to Christ as King must expect to find that there are many aspects of its corporate life which it cannot tie up quite so neatly as some prosaic minds would wish.

Certainly the call to the ministry is not felt only by those who have lived within the worshipping life of the church since their earliest days. Far from it. It can come to those who have ranged widely, tried everything once, and have fought their way through to faith the hard way. Of such, for example, was St. Augustine of Hippo.

The requirements of baptism and confirmation also imply, as well as commitment to Christ within a living historical society, a recognition of certain if limited truths concerning the nature of reality itself. In other words they presuppose that the worship, the biblicism, the credal statements of the church, point finally to an 'ontology'. Christianity is not just a vague sentimentality; the projection of a man's longings out upon a non-existent, if wished for, reality. Christian Faith has particular content. It endeavours to witness to the truth that sets a man free, no matter how much in this endeavour it may have to strain the resources of language, and dig down deeply, to discover new metaphors.

(2) SELECTION

So far, this chapter has, in the main, been concerned with the call, the inner constraint, which prompts a man to offer himself for the ministry. Yet if this is to lead to, and realise itself in ordination, this call must be reinforced by the judgment of the church, the Christian community, which sets its seal upon it. The prophet *per se* needs no authority or recognition, other than his own strong sense of vocation, and that which is implicit in the nature of the message which he forthtells. He knows that he must utter it if he is to be true both to himself and to that which constrains him. Status or official recognition would often embarrass him. Did not George III in this context cynically regret that he had not made John Wesley a bishop? But the call to the priesthood cannot be validated in quite this way, for being a priest is to exercise a particular office and assume a status within a given historical community. This community has a shape, a structure, a continuing and controlled existence. The priest contributes to its life and through Christ draws life and authority from it. He expresses that society not simply by what he says, but by what he is and what he does. A man may have a great desire to build the Kingdom of God, to commit himself to Christ, to give himself in service to his fellow men. He may go further and come to the conviction that being the person he is, with the particular experience into which he has entered, he can most effectively do this as a priest. It does not necessarily follow, however, that in this he is right. His contribution may perhaps better be made, in view of his abilities and opportunities, within the context of his present niche in society and his occupation as factory worker, technician, barrister or schoolmaster.

Thus two decisions have to be made. The first by the individual person himself as to whether, in response to what seems to him a compulsion, a call to duty, he should offer himself for the ministry. The second, by the church, as to whether in the case of this person his sense of a call ought to lead to ordination.

There is, of course, ambiguity here, almost a seeming contradiction, as all too often in human affairs. The individual person may well feel that he alone can know and assess what is happening within him: whilst the historical community must equally claim the right to decide who shall be its accredited ministers. Such a tension cannot be resolved by any application of a formal logic: only in life, and then through humility and by a recognition that there are diversities of gifts and functions—and that both individuals and institutions make mistakes.

In practice, then, selection for the ministry cannot in the nature of the case be entirely self-selection, no matter how strong the individual's conviction that he has a real vocation. Called he may be, but not necessarily to the priesthood. Anyhow, it is a good thing to submit ourselves, at times, to the judgment of our fellows, though this does not necessarily mean that they are always right, or our own judgment, where it runs counter to the corporate decision, is always wrong. There are no infallibilities in human affairs, and divine treasures must be contained within earthen vessels. We must make the best judgment that we can, believing that integrity, intelligence, and a humble willingness to seek guidance will at least lead us towards right decisions.

By what process, then, does the church select its priests from those who offer themselves?

The first answer is that responsibility for ordination finally rests with the bishop of the diocese, and until well on in this century he made the selection either personally or through his chaplains. In the seventeenth and eighteenth centuries the examination simply took the form of answering a few questions (in Latin) on the Thirty-Nine Articles of Religion from the Book of Common Prayer, preceded or followed by an interview with the bishop, when the candidate exhibited his testimonials, one of which, if he were a graduate, was from his college. It was rare for a young man to be turned down, though I know from my own researches that this did at times happen, usually because of political disloyalty or sheer intellectual incapacity. The procedure leading to ordination was then all very simple, the assumption being that here was a sphere of useful and worth-while service, and that any competent and well disposed person who sought it ought to go forward. It was in this respect a profession.

There is much to be said for such intimacy of ordinand and bishop (when it works) though its defects are, perhaps, obvious. Too much responsibility is placed in the hands of one man (i.e. the bishop) who may not have the particular gifts which measure up to this assignment. Also it can lead to a too indivi-dual assessment arising out of particular diocesan needs. Such a method can, of course, be gloriously right, the more so where the bishop seeks advice widely: but it suffers from the fact that there is no effective lay element necessarily built into its structure of selection.

There is, of course, no ideally right technique of selection as many institutions have discovered sometimes to their cost. Every system has its merits but cannot entirely eliminate its short-comings.

To-day the selection of candidates for ordination, where such candidates are under forty years of age and sometimes when they are over, is for all practical purposes in the hands of the Central Advisory Council for the Ministry. This body was set up by the bishops in 1913 as the Central Advisory Council on Training for the Ministry, and was renamed and reconstituted by the Church Assembly in 1959. To this body, while not

surrendering their final authority, the bishops have now volun-
tarily entrusted their responsibility.

This means, in practice, that a man who offers himself for the
ministry, whether he approaches his parish priest (this is a
usual first step) or however he sets about it, is finally referred to
C.A.C.T.M. It is not usual, though C.A.C.T.M. holds conferences for schoolboys in part to foster a vocation, for a young man
to go before a selection conference until he is eighteen years of
age. The procedure then is that after references and testimonials
have been taken up, enquiries made, and interviews held with a
C.A.C.T.M. secretary, the prospective ordinand goes to a
conference. These are held in various parts of the country, and
last some four days. The conference consists usually of five
selectors, including one or two lay people, and there may be as
many as twenty candidates present. They all live together, so
that there is time for informal talk and get-togethers, and each
selector sees the candidate privately. Finally a considered report
on each man is sent to the bishop, and the candidate is, or is not,
recommended for training—and usually suggestions are made as
to the nature of the training which will suit him best. The
decision is never final and absolute, because the candidate can
ask at some future date to go to another conference. Indeed the
suggestion is often made that he should do this. There is also
the bishop in the background.

The selection conference seeks to judge not so much present
achievement as potential promise, what the candidate has it in
him to become, given the environment and opportunity to
bring it out, rather than what at the moment he is. Its members, moreover, have to think in terms of what the priesthood
implies and demands in the particular situation of the Church
of England now, remembering that its task is by no means
confined to priestly and representative acts within patterns of
worship in church. The conferences must place the priest and his
work within a wide context of past history and contemporary
need. In this respect their assignment is made somewhat more
difficult since there are specialised functions within the ordained
ministry (for example teaching) for which a man might well be
suitable but which do not demand the same aptitudes as are

required in the parish priest. By and large, however, it is the latter category which the selectors have in mind, sometimes it may be without conscious intention. Certainly this priority would rightly tend to be uppermost in the minds of the lay members.

If this is true, what in particular are the selectors looking for? As suggested earlier they are endeavouring to make some total assessment of the person in terms of potential and promise, in particular in relation to the life-commitment of a parish priest. A man may have had little formal education, but he may have outstanding gifts, and be capable of acquiring such general and specific knowledge as is necessary. A man, again, may have hitherto moved very little in 'church circles', but this could prove a positive asset, for he may well bring with him a breath of fresh air where it is much needed.

Certain obvious gifts the C.A.C.T.M. selectors must look for when they are thinking in terms of the parish priest, such as, for example, the capacity to lead. I shall defer discussion of this necessary requirement to a subsequent chapter, but it must be stressed here and now that whether he wishes it or not an incumbent is in a position where he must exercise leadership. It is expected of him—and if he does not give it no-one else easily can or will. Perhaps this implies a criticism of the Anglican parochial system, and suggests that in this respect the Church of England clergy stand in a different relation than the Free Churches to their lay people. I think this is probably true. It is, therefore, tragic when a priest goes to a parish and it soon becomes apparent, to others if not to himself, that he would never be there in such a position of leadership if he had been left to find his own level in another walk of life.

Integrity and a sincere Christian conviction are also essential, for without these the priest will not get very far, and whatever abilities he has will lack a unitary dedication. Intelligence and commonsense, the latter in particular—they do not necessarily go together—are of course important. Essential also is depth in a person, such depth being the product of an interior life constantly renewed. Certainly the priest ought to be seen to have 'got something', and that 'something' to have a

Godward reference or dimension. Nor must we forget a sense of humour, which often relieves tedium, begets charity, and prevents unnecessary anger. Nothing more effectively deflates pomposity. It is a good thing, at times, to be able to laugh at ourselves. Other people will, anyhow!

But a catalogue of this kind, listing endowments in propositional form, and giving marks accordingly, doesn't somehow add up to making a balanced assessment of a whole person. People are more subtle and more complex than this. They are greater than the sum total of their parts. Ultimately, I suppose, it is a matter of whether a man is really alive in himself, whether he continues to grow, is still curious about existence, capable of wonder, rooting himself more firmly in reality and truth as the years go by.

There is, however, one essential in the priest, to which I must call particular attention, since in the nature of things he must be first and foremost a pastor. I refer to the capacity to enter into free, mature and effective personal relations. The sad fact is that many people, it may be through some unresolved inner conflict, are not prepared to expose themselves as persons to their fellow men. Their awareness of the other man is part of a distorted self-awareness. They shrink from any frank revelation of themselves. They parade a false and often self-justifying image and it is this projection which vitiates their personal relations at the root. No real encounter results from their meeting with people. There is no dialogue, no creative tension, no *rapport*. Such people convert what ought to be a 'going forth' to others into a self-regarding soliloquy. They are 'cribbed, cabined and confined' within a self-constructed prison house and as a consequence they either become aggressive, or, in reverse, keep themselves very much to themselves. They neither know nor are known, for it is only in relationships of mutual trust that persons grow and move on to final commitments of love.

This matter of personal relations is important, for religion is itself relationship. God so loved the world that He gave—not a blue-print of the mechanics of salvation but a son, a person. Commitment to Jesus expresses itself in commitment to other people and this means respecting their integrity and uniqueness.

It is only, I repeat, in our willingness to be ourselves in our relations with each other that we are born into loving. Thus the tragedy with far too many of us is that our personal relations are formal only: they do not embody a real encounter but are confined, often within class structures, to the niceties and conventions of a routine operation. How often one hears it said, and how pathetic: 'I just can't get to know him.' When it is the vicar who merits the remark, pathos moves over into tragedy.

I have somewhat spread myself here because I believe that the capacity and preparedness to enter into really effective personal relations is the *sine qua non* of the true pastor. Without this much of his ministry will be in vain. Entering into relations with people is something more than a concern for them, because it demands the laying bare of ourselves. It requires the shedding of false pride, the acceptance of ourselves and others as we and they are, being willing to learn from them as we hope they may learn from us. To make this possible, something has got to happen in a man, so that from out of his own release, that is because he is released, he ceases to wish to blitz, to manipulate, to control his neighbours. There is always a subtle temptation for the priest to do precisely this. The liberated man recognises that every personal relationship constitutes a unique event. A person is not simply one of a kind, a representative object, a substance which thinks, though a judge in an assize court may have to reckon in terms of that fiction of the legal mind 'the reasonable man'. A person is himself in a unique way, but he is only himself in relation with others equally unique—that is within a personal order, a community.

It is a deep awareness of this truth, and a willingness to 'know' people in such a way, that constitute the prerequisite of the good pastor. It is not only, to use old-fashioned terminology, being a 'lover of souls', but of releasing and recreating oneself in the act of loving. This is different from the master-disciple relationship, though it can be inclusive of it. A pastor who is not genuinely interested in and fascinated by the human scene will find boredom where he ought to meet stimulus and be provoked into excitement. He will become involved, in the wrong way, in a self-regarding way, with those to whom he ministers.

It is not always easy for a C.A.C.T.M. conference to find out whether the potential to minister to people in this way—that is by entering into effective personal relations with them—exists in the candidate. Perhaps the conference will discover this only if its own members are themselves sufficiently liberated and are thus able to evoke an equal liberation in others, where it exists potentially. The selection of the selectors is certainly very important!

But to return to the conferences themselves. The criticism often made of corporate decisions is that on the whole they tend to be prudential and unimaginative: the choice is geared down to the pace of the slowest vessel in the convoy. The unusual or exceptional man, so it is said, seldom appeals to everybody, whereas the more ordinary and pedestrian person is reassuring, and creates, in the group mind, the mood: 'We can't go wrong with him.' This possible weakness in corporate decisions has to be recognised if only that it may be overcome. That C.A.C.T.M. conferences make mistakes of this kind is of course certain. No judgment, in its nature so delicate, can hope to avoid error when it is undertaken by fallible men, the more so when it is often geared to promise rather than to performance. The question is not whether C.A.C.T.M. makes mistakes but whether its conferences tend to make fewer mistakes than an older method or an alternative which might be devised. On the whole this modest claim may (I think) be allowed it though this assertion is, of course, as incapable of proof as of disproof. Responsible opinion would probably assert and (I think) rightly that C.A.C.T.M. has raised the general standard of the men in the ministry, even if now and again an exceptional person has slipped through its fingers. Also the method itself inspires confidence and is seen to be fair, just and impartial. As a safeguard there is always the bishop in the background who, if he is willing to take his courage in both hands, can use an absolute discretion. The very existence of such a final authority may help to secure the best of both worlds.

Any criticism of the method has, of course, to recognise that selection can only be undertaken from those who elect to come forward. The perfect ordinand is laid up in Heaven and even C.A.C.T.M. will not persuade him to come down.

I want at this point to say something of the ordination of older men—that is of men over forty—a matter on which I feel strongly. Here the bishop may send them to C.A.C.T.M. or not as he pleases. It is usually a help to such men (though perhaps not always) to attend a selection conference alongside the other candidates. The decision as to a man's fitness and the kind of training he should do still rests with the bishop. It is not a good thing that everyone should go through the same mill; nor is a theological college by any means always the right environment for everybody. What is wanted, as I suggested earlier, is a diversity of approach to this important matter of recruitment and training. The older man has certain positive advantages.

First he comes to his ministry with a wide experience often gained the hard way. He has had to meet his fellow men at their own level, an important conditioning factor, since one of the most difficult problems confronting the *young* clergyman is that he often tends to evoke a stylised, artificial and formal reaction to himself and is not sufficiently experienced to do much to offset this. The clerical collar can both deaden and impoverish the impact of his personal encounters.

Secondly, the older man will probably avoid the feeling of staleness which can all too easily oppress the long established clergyman in middle life, when experience may seem to lose its cutting edge. True, this acidity can be avoided if he is the kind of man who continues to learn, and draws more deeply as the years go on from the wells which really do contain living water. But the fact remains that the young man who is ordained in his middle twenties needs to be a 'big man' if he is to move steadily forward and is not to undergo a period of great personal strain when he comes to his fifties. To be forewarned can help in being forearmed. Familiarity with holy things undoubtedly exposes a man to an enormous strain. Perhaps a year off duty would be the answer—in part!

The older man, however, is far less likely to be the victim of this kind of staleness. When the clergyman once young but now old is beginning to slow down, he is beginning to gear up. Other difficulties, of course, come his way, but not this one in particular.

Thirdly, and for the same reason, the older man can avoid some of the professionalism which is almost inevitable when a person has been a long time in the same occupation. Indeed a measure of professionalism is useful, for it can add to efficiency, avoid fuss, and reduce nervous strain. It can also render less offensive some personal idiosyncrasies. But an excess of professionalism in a clergyman can be particularly nauseating, for it makes what ought to be a unique occasion into a routine operation. At all costs the older man must resist the pressures to professionalism which will be brought to bear upon him, both at his theological college (if he goes to one), and subsequently by the congregation in the church he serves. The particular contribution which he has to offer will be in part vitiated if he assumes the veneer of a professionalism which does not really belong to him. True he may remain too much the schoolmaster, too much the colonel, and retain too many traces of his former career. This can be a limitation, but it is far better than an artificially assumed clerical guise.

Fourthly, the older man also has the advantage of having learnt a technique of working. This is particularly important in view of the fact that the parish priest has to galvanise himself into action: his urge to sustained labour must come from within, and for many men this is asking a great deal, particularly as the years go by.

Finally, it is important to add that the older ordinand must not be thought of as a second best, as a desperate resort to remedy a shortage of recruits. It is not necessarily a matter for regret that he did not experience or respond to a sense of vocation earlier. Far from it: for he is now able to make his own contribution through a specialised experience in other fields. Many clergy (myself included!) would have benefited from a wider acquaintance with men and affairs in an exposed environment. A clergyman's life is a tough one: the world can toughen him up for it. A case could perhaps the more easily be made against the ordination of men under thirty than it could be for a refusal to ordain after forty.

But there is, of course, no need to make such a case, for the church needs in its ministry those who come to it early as well as those who come to it late. The priesthood is undoubtedly enriched by the young and enthusiastic; by those who under the pressure of a youthful idealism and, fortunately, not having yet learnt prudence, dare to make mistakes. It is usually the young who are in a hurry: it is the old (with the significant exception of Pope John) who think that they have all the time in the world on their hands and can, therefore, afford to wait. A parish is fortunate if every now and again there comes into it one who seeks to take the Kingdom of God by storm. People need waking up and the young are often best fitted to do this. Congregations usually take it better from them. If, as I believe it ought to, the Church of England should more and more encourage its clergy to do a period of service overseas, then it is the young who are more likely to hear, and can most easily respond to, this call.

For the married ordinand, whether old or young (and the tendency is towards younger marriage), it is essential that the wife should be 'with' him in this adventure. If she is indifferent to it, or in her heart resentful, then his ministry will be exposed to exceptional difficulty and intolerable strain. In such circumstances he will be well advised not to go forward.

I have tried to suggest, in this chapter, that recruitment to the ministry of the church should be broadly based and widely spread in every way. There is room in its ranks for the once born and the twice born; for the man who has lived his life on an even keel, and for the man who has sowed his wild oats and has won through to faith. There is room in its ranks for men from all social strata (so long as such strata exist); for men from different educational backgrounds; for great diversities of gifts and temperament; for the married and the unmarried; the older and the younger. But such men, in so far as it is the parochial ministry that is in mind, must have a capacity for leadership, and be capable of entering into free and effective relations with people.

Only such a ministry will succeed in planting the Christian gospel in the rich and varied soil of contemporary England.

(3) TRAINING

It is time now to ask how the selected candidate is trained for the ministry that he is later to undertake. Until the nineteenth century there was no specialised training as such for the clergy. It was not thought necessary and for many reasons. Among these was the fact that the universities were largely religious foundations, and one of their main objects was to produce fit persons to serve God in church and state—and this was understood as including ministers of religion within the Church of England. Subscription to the Thirty-Nine Articles was obligatory either before registering as a student or on receiving a degree. Divinity formed a necessary part of the curriculum for everyone. Most fellowships could only be held by ordained clergymen of the Church of England.

Bishops, therefore, tried to insist, in post-reformation England, that all clergymen should obtain a degree at one of the universities (Oxford, Cambridge and Trinity College, Dublin). In practice it did not always work out this way: but within a context in which church and state were regarded in some sense at least as one and indivisible—the toleration granted to nonconformists in 1689 was merely a toleration—the teaching given by the universities was regarded as adequate. A parson in the late eighteenth-century was for the most part a country gentleman with specialised functions: and for the latter a knowledge of the Bible and Thirty-Nine Articles of Religion, a little church history, and of course familiarity with the Book of Common Prayer (together, at the turn of the century, with a reading of Paley's *Evidences*)—these were all that were regarded as essential. In the same way as the English came to have a horror of a standing professional army because of their sufferings under Cromwell's major-generals during the Commonwealth, so they entertained a horror of the seminary priest, the mass-priest of Rome, who was in his own line of country a professional. They felt more at home, and not entirely for the wrong reasons, with the more amateur Anglican parson, ensconced with his wife and large family in the rectory. They understood him and he felt that he understood them. Anti-clericalism of the kind which has proved so devastating a political force on the continent of Europe has been almost unknown in our own country.

The nineteenth century, however, brought new needs and fresh challenges. The assumption that all citizens were Anglicans, even Christians, was seen to be no longer tenable. The universities were becoming (to use an unhappy and much misunderstood modern term) secularised. The professions, medicine, for example, were entering upon a period of greater specialisation. Training for them was lengthened and was becoming far more empirical in character. New secular and explosive ideologies were agitating Europe and many people openly avowed themselves anti-Christian. Great social and political movements were being born, and science was seen by many as a new religion of humanity.

It was impossible for the Christian church, which because of its belief in incarnation had integrated itself with the very fabric of western Europe, to be unaffected by these tumultuous events. In England the first reaction of the national church, after its organisational reform by Parliament, and under the impetus of the Oxford Movement, was to rediscover itself, with its own particular history, as a continuing branch of the universal catholic church. Its later reaction under the leadership of such men as Maurice, Westcott, Hort and Gore was to try to incarnate itself anew in the changing social and political scene, and to commend its Gospel within the thought forms generated by the flooding in of new knowledge.

The result was a growing conviction that for the clergy a greater degree of technical training was essential, a training in which the curriculum and the whole intention could be geared to the equipping of a priest for his pastoral and sacrificial task in the contemporary world. If he were to minister effectively to modern man, subjected as modern man was to new conditioning and environmental pressures—pressures which to-day have become even more acute—then it was necessary to add to the 'flair' of the gifted amateur a greater expertise in matters pastoral, theological, and liturgical.

Thus there was founded at Birmingham in 1828 the first theological training college in England. To-day there are some twenty-seven of them situated up and down the country, all having arisen spontaneously and remaining independent, each with its own governing body and brand of churchmanship. By and large they are small communities of some thirty to fifty men, each under a principal with some three or four other members of staff, all of whom are clergymen. Indeed the training of priests is clerically dominated.

The task of these colleges is twofold: to equip the ordinands, of whom the vast proportion will become parish priests, with the specialised knowledge necessary for the discharge of their duties, and at the same time to foster in them the disciplined spiritual life. No priest, no matter how gifted and devout, can expect to undertake his responsibilities in the contemporary world by the light of nature alone. To lead worship, to act as the focal point of a community, to live out a Christ-loyalty and to encourage it in others, to be sensitive to people in their needs both individual and corporate—these demand a practical skill, a measure of specialised 'know how'. Christian Faith, it must be stressed again, has a particular content, since commitment to Jesus presupposes a great deal as to man's nature—what he is like—and how his fulfilment can be brought about. It may not always be easy to express these truths in propositional form, but the effort to state their implications must none the less be made. There is of necessity a built-in place for a theology of the right kind, bearing witness to a Christian Faith which is not just a kind of pious uplift, rootless, unrelated to an objective reality, incapable of intelligent statement. If what this Faith tries to say shades off into mystery; if the language which it uses is always inadequate to contain the reality to which it refers; if its dedication to Christ is constantly struggling to express itself in new forms and within different situational contexts; yet there remains a 'givenness' about it. A clergyman, in his parish, is not there simply as an intelligent person of good-will—we hope that he is this and unless he is he will not get very far—but he is also an accredited, i.e. commissioned representative of an historic community, mediating and challenging men with a particular way of life. Hence the overriding need for a specific kind of training.

It is for the purpose of securing this that the theological college exists.

It is important to notice that when a young man is approved by C.A.C.T.M. as an ordinand, he is usually urged to take a degree before going to a theological college, and only if it is thought that he would find this too exacting is the advice not offered. The degree can be in any subject and, from the point of view of the ministry as a whole, it is a good thing that such a degree should not be confined to theology, although C.A.C.T.M. usually encourages most candidates to read at least some theology during their study at the university.

There are several alternative courses for candidates under the age of twenty-five who do not qualify for a university degree. Students at King's College, London, which is the largest theological faculty in the country, and at the London College of Divinity, can read for an Associateship of the College; this is both a theological and professional course of study. Kelham runs a special comprehensive course for non-graduates. Others take a course of pre-theological study of the humanities at Brasted or the Bernard Gilpin Society, Durham, before going on to a theological college. The minimum educational standard for these last courses is five 'O' level subjects in G.C.E., unless a man is specially selected for Brasted; but it is possible that this standard may be raised to include one 'A' level subject before long.

Most students at theological colleges take a course in preparation for what is called the General Ordination Examination. This is spread over a period of two years for graduates and men over the age of thirty; otherwise it takes three years. The subjects for study include the Bible (both Old and New Testaments), Greek, Church History, the Book of Common Prayer, Liturgy, Christian Doctrine, Pastoralia,* Ethics

---

* This includes elementary psychology and what the Americans call 'counselling'. There can be little doubt that the study of Pastoralia has suffered from the decline of interest in moral theology, which it is hoped may be revived.

(recently restored to the syllabus of subjects examined) and Elocution.

It is sometimes complained that the syllabus of G.O.E. is too wide, in that it introduces the student to little bits of many things, thereby only scratching the surface and never stretching the mind. Thus, it is said, the standard of attainment required is low. On the other hand it might be claimed that the breadth of the curriculum helps to correct the tendency of small colleges to a somewhat psychologically intense introversion, particularly dangerous in a religious society.

How far the curriculum is best adapted to the training of a parish priest has often been questioned, but the practical problem has always been to replace it with a better. Working for G.O.E. does not, of course, stand alone, because preparation for it is set within the context of a total life which includes daily worship and prayer, sport and recreation, and the direct encounter of man with man that such living together in small communities makes possible. Special courses, visiting speakers and group activities during the vacations open windows upon the outer world.

Perhaps the most serious criticism of such training is that the theological college does little of significance to prepare a man to live and work within the highly industrialised, technological society in which his ministry will largely be exercised. The importance of the economic structures which this society generates, and their influence upon the industrial worker, can hardly be exaggerated. Yet if truth must be told, many an ordinand at the end of his training sees such structures as alien and strange. Most theological colleges simply have not got members of staff equipped to face up to this situation; and the very geographical location of some colleges prevents any psychological intrusion from this somewhat austere world outside.

The bishops and those responsible for the training of ordinands are, of course, well aware of these and other related problems. Indeed one of the most hopeful 'signs of the times' in this respect is the readiness of the church, for example through C.A.C.T.M.'s Theological Education Committee, to engage in a dialogue and to be self-critical. The new emphasis to be placed on ethics as a subject of study, and the fact that Birmingham University, through the initiative of sociologists, doctors and clergy, has instituted a 'Diploma in Pastoral Studies' may well point the way forward.

Training, of course, must include certain courses. Everyone agrees that the priest needs to know the scriptures and be familiar with their essential thought forms. The problem is their communication in our modern age. What ought to be equally agreed is that the ordinand should be informed as to the essential content of other world Faiths and be introduced into a new and more enlightened (indeed humble!) attitude towards them. The encounter of these Faiths with each other will undoubtedly lead to one of the most creative dialogues in the contemporary scene and one which will become increasingly important. The fact is that it is no longer possible, even if it were thought desirable, to seal off Christianity from the richly religious world around it.

Equally important is it that the young ordinand should be given some simple philosophical training. Philosophy asks, or ought to ask, the perennial questions which necessarily arise from every man's experience. At a time when the sciences loom ever larger and knowledge is becoming more specialised and fragmented, it is of overriding importance that people in general, and the clergyman in particular, should be able to speak a common language.

Most theological colleges, fortunately, manage to secure fairly exciting principals—we must not forget their wives who constitute a uniquely helpful 'ingredient'—and this is of the highest importance in small communities. The principal is in a position to lay down the overall pattern, to exercise effective leadership, and in some indefinable way to give atmosphere to the whole. The difficulty of recruiting other staff of an equally high calibre, however, is at times reflected by a measure of dullness and lack of inspiration in both lecture rooms and tutorials.

A potentially stimulating ingredient in such colleges may well be found in the future in a wider spread in the social background of the ordinands, though at present the general ethos is still predominantly respectable and middle-class. It is of interest to note that of the men ordained deacon in 1963 just over 50 per cent were graduates, 22 per cent being from Oxford and Cambridge and 28 per cent from other universities. About 35 per cent of the men at theological colleges have been to independent (i.e. public) schools; 24 per cent are over thirty years of age when they are recommended for training; and 36 per cent of the men at theological colleges are married. Of those who have come straight from university, some have been abroad, probably immediately after leaving school. A large minority of the total ordinands have done other work in a wide variety of fields. The number from (to use an old-fashioned nomenclature) the industrial working classes is lamentably small, a fact which must be deplored, but which is symptomatic of a serious contemporary religious and social situation—a subject to which we shall return. This also links up with what was said earlier about training.

Theological colleges differ among themselves in their general ethos and kind of churchmanship, since their independent origins reflect various traditions within the Church of England. Taken as a whole and particularly when seen by a tidy mind, the existence of some twenty-seven small colleges may seem wasteful of manpower and grossly uneconomic—and in some respects this is true.

It may be questioned, however, whether its lack of logic, even with the defects that go along with this, does not in practice make it more flexible and capable of catering for the needs of individual men, thereby adding considerably to the life and vitality of the church. At least the system—it isn't really a system—does enable the ordinand to exercise a real choice as to where he is to go; and the smallness of the unit makes for and demands effective personal relations. The naturally shy man will more easily find his feet and, as we say, have to 'come out'. The strongly individualised person is more readily assimilated in the small rather than in the large group.

The weakness of the present situation lies in the great demands that it makes on the church for adequate and exciting teaching staff, particularly where any high-level tuition is required—and this at a time when it is difficult to attract into this work enough first-class and vital men. Finally, a college is what the staff make it. Obviously it would be cheaper and less prodigal of teaching talent to have fewer and larger colleges, including a large comprehensive one, which could be broken down into houses catering for different educational streams! The need for a greater number of high-level lecturers could in part, however, be met by siting colleges in the new university towns and making more use of the facilities thus made available. This would also help to correct an almost inevitable introversion. Maybe one or two large theological colleges existing alongside the smaller might be a possible solution.

But here, as elsewhere, the perfect system is laid up in Heaven, and I am not at all convinced that the small college, expensive as it is, has not more to offer in view of the many-sided nature of the 'job' it is trying to do, and the historically comprehensive character of the Church of England. Perhaps the answer is that a number of approaches to this problem is needed, and that it is wise to avoid getting bogged down in a rigid overall system. If the view is taken—and I myself do take this view—that the varieties of churchmanship and outlook which obtain within the Church of England add enormously to its corporate and witnessing life, since the truth is greater than them all put together, then the small college with its measure of independence may well be justified and worth the additional cost. The very existence of diversity in this field invites comparison, encourages the best kind of emulation, and provokes criticism. Concentrations of power, particularly over the mind, can be dangerous. Dr. Vidler, when he was at Windsor, trained a few men for the ministry in his own house, and when he left for Cambridge this creative experiment, which depended upon his own unique flair, lapsed. Canon Armstrong has founded a college for older men at Worcester, and the Southwark diocese under Canon Stanley Evans, has now started an ordination training course which makes it possible for men working in the day-time to do their studies in the evening. Experimentation of this kind is invaluable; and the more individual initiative can be encouraged, the more new life and vitality will flow into the church. Old institutions need constantly to be given a new look; methods of training submitted to criticism and periodical review.

In stressing the individual origin of English theological colleges, it must be added that their independence, in practical terms, has been diminished, for example, in respect of admissions, by their financial dependence on the Central Advisory Council for the Ministry. This Council has an overall responsibility for the selection and training of ordinands; administers the money which the parishes and dioceses raise for this purpose; and from time to time inspects the colleges and sends a report on them to the bishops. Such a system is inevitably bound to mean (no matter how indirect and concealed) a measure of control, for no college can manage to survive financially on its present endowments at a time when students do not pay their own way. Such a *via media* may, however, help to get the best of both worlds—final overall direction with a reasonable individual liberty.

Mention has already been made of the older ordinand, and the setting up of special institutions for him. It may well be questioned, however, how far the theological college is for him at all. Its corporate and *quasi* academic life can serve to blunt the edge of natural aptitude without replacing it with a conscious expertise, rather in the same way as a little psychology can be the ruination of parents (and teachers) in so far as it saps their confidence. Though the older man may be more mature as a person than his younger colleagues (and in this sense adds to the life of the collegiate community) his inability to be equally articulate, or fluent in the use of the written word, can add up to making him less sure of himself just when he ought not to be in such a state of uncertainty. He needs all the encouragement he can get.

Perhaps this means that different patterns of training are necessary: and that for some older people to be put under the care of one man might be the best practical introduction to the priesthood. There is, in addition, something unnatural in removing an older ordinand from his home and family and subjecting him to a routine which is more easily assimilable when a man comes to it young. It must in fairness be added, however, that many principals are sensitive to the needs of the older married men, and that often the wife lives near the college.

To suggest, however, that he need not go to college does not mean for a single moment that there is no need for him, with all ordinands, to cultivate habits of regular prayer, and to be trained in the technique and 'know how' of such a cultivation. Indeed in so far as western Europe is a sick society, it may well be that this is because its activist philosophy of living is not sustained by a disciplined cultivation of that Reality, the living God, which is beyond and within. Yet the learning of this necessary skill does not demand a college or lecture room. It can be fostered elsewhere—but fostered it must be if the priest is to lead his people in prayer, pray for them, and himself be a man of both vision and power.

CHAPTER 3

SETTING OUT ON HIS MINISTRY

(1) ASSISTANT CURATE

AFTER selection and training comes ordination, most frequently in a cathedral but sometimes in a parish church, first as deacon and then as priest. In the Church of England this can only be done by a bishop, usually of the diocese in which the new deacon or priest is to serve, since ordination nearly always goes along with an episcopal licence to undertake a pastoral responsibility in a cure of souls, that is in a parish. The distinction between what is called the diaconate and the priesthood need not, in a book of this kind, detain us, for the former status is now invariably the prelude to ordination as a priest, the latter usually following a year after. Each step, it may be noticed—and this is the relic of an older system—is preceded by the diocese's own examination usually on the Bible and the Book of Common Prayer: but it is unusual for the ordinand, who has successfully negotiated previous hurdles, to fail at either of these. Though in theory reference is constantly made to the three-fold ministry of bishop, priest and deacon, in practice only the first two are now permanent ingredients in the ordained ministry of the Church of England. The retention of the diaconate for a probationary year—a deacon does not celebrate the Holy Communion—has the advantage of initiating the new clergyman gradually into his full duties. The wise vicar uses this period to encourage him to continue with his reading and does not ask him to preach too often. As it is, most dioceses extend the training of their younger clergy, under the direction of an experienced priest, for a period of some three years. Whether the office of deacon will or ought to be revived in any effective sense, particularly in respect of men working in the everyday world, has often been debated, but so far little has been done.

The essential requirement for ordination, as we have already seen, is that the ordinand himself has experienced an inner constraint which has brought him to where he is. When made deacon he professes his belief that he is 'inwardly moved by the Holy Ghost': and at his ordination to the priesthood that he is 'truly called'. As part of his own declaration of faith he also affirms his conviction as to the unique authority of the scriptures; his intention to study and teach from them; and to try to fashion his own life, together with that of his family, 'according to the Doctrine of Christ', setting 'forwards . . . quietness, peace and love among all Christian people, and especially among them that are or shall be committed to (his) charge'.

Upon making his own profession of faith in this way, and after the invocation of the Spirit, he is ordained priest by the bishop placing both hands on his head (the other priests present doing the same) and pronouncing the words: 'Receive the Holy Ghost for the Office and Work of a Priest in the Church of God.' This is followed by the bishop giving him 'Authority to preach the Word of God, and to minister the holy Sacraments in the Congregation'. The bishop is here acting on behalf of the Christian community, and mediating through Christ to the newly ordained (so Christians believe) the grace of God for this special ministry.

The ordained priest now becomes a minister in the Church of God, but the particular sphere in which he is commissioned to discharge his ministry, for the time being at least, is within the Church of this realm. This national or local character is reflected in his being required to subscribe to the Thirty-Nine Articles of Religion; and to testify, in respect of the Book of Common Prayer with its 'Making, Ordaining and Consecrating of Bishops, Priests, and Deacons' that the doctrine set forth therein is 'agreeable to the Word of God' and that he will 'use the form prescribed in the said book and none other except so far as shall be ordered by lawful authority'. He also takes the oath of allegiance to the Crown and swears canonical obedience to his bishop.

The need to subscribe to the Thirty-Nine Articles has recently come under fire and certainly with a considerable show of reason. These Articles constitute a Reformation Profession of Faith, and reflect the religious struggles and questionings of that period. Calvinist in tone, they are, it is true, surprisingly liberal when compared with similar documents coming out of the same historical situation. Few clergymen could conscientiously subscribe to each Article in particular, but the assent required under the Clerical Subscription Act of 1865 is general in character and this goes some way to relieve many consciences. Such assent is also required from an incumbent upon his induction to a parish. Indeed on this occasion it is more than assent, for he must read the Articles in church.

The wisdom of such a requirement, to say nothing of its rightness, is very questionable. Though some may see such subscription as necessarily (if unfortunately) involved in the ministry of a Church which has its own particular history— there is always a tension between the individual and the community—the present position is far from satisfactory. Integrity and intellectual honesty do matter, and it is not a good thing, when a man sets out on his ministry, to encourage mental gymnastics or reservations. It is to be hoped that some relief will be offered in this matter.

Ordination to the diaconate, as we have seen, almost invariably goes along with the licensing as an assistant curate to a parochial cure, that is to a definite pastoral responsibility in the Church of England. This leads to the question: By what process does the newly made deacon go to a particular parish?

The answer is that he goes there by no necessary or absolute direction: it is left to him, after such advice as he may seek, to make up his own mind. Suggestions as to where he ought to go may well be made to him by the bishop, by the head of his theological college, by a friend: or he may see an advertisement in a church newspaper and on his own initiative make an application.

Some critics feel that there ought to be more direction in this matter, perhaps by the bishop, as in the American church, during the first few years of a man's ministry: or, if not direction, that a greater influence ought to be brought to bear upon the newly ordained to ensure that they go to the 'right' parish. Certainly something is needed to secure a more coherent and economic utilisation of a limited personnel. It is true, for example, that there is a marked tendency for curacies to be sought in the south rather than in the north; for the salubrious parts of the country to prove more attractive to somewhat un-enterprising men than areas which are tougher, industrial, and as a consequence more challenging. As evidence of this it is pointed out that certain parishes, in relation to the present supply of clergy and the demands made upon them, are over-staffed, while some vaster parishes of over ten thousand are under-staffed—indeed are often left in the hands of one struggl-ing incumbent.

It is, of course, in relation to such facts that a case for a measure of direction is strongest.

The matter, however, is not quite so simple as it at first seems, in particular when it is a question of seeking a title. Here, any form of direction must take account of the total situation.

A young man, with some forty years of active ministry before him, may properly regard his first three or four years as an apprenticeship. This means in effect that what he should be looking for is not necessarily the parish in which the need for manpower is greatest, but the parish where he can gain the most valuable experience, and receive from the incumbent the best possible training. There is all the difference in the world between being an assistant curate, working under another man, and having final responsibility for the care of the parish. Such responsibility means not only giving total direction, but taking a stand, sometimes making unpopular decisions, and living with the results of them. The assistant curate is in part protected from exposure to the full rigours of such a situation.

The fact is that certain parishes are not suitable as training grounds for the newly ordained, for they are either too eccentri-cally individual, too challenging or too comfortable. In addition to this, not every incumbent is capable of training a priest in his early years. He may lack the right temperament or not be sufficiently skilled himself. To live and let live, and yet at the same time to give proper direction, is not within the competence of every man. To encourage a young curate to stand on his own feet while at the same time protecting him from the crippling weight of excessive responsibility, this demands great understanding. Though certain parishes by their very nature are not and cannot be made fitting training grounds, finally it is the man that is more significant: it is the right vicar who matters most.

The relationship between incumbent and assistant curate is ambiguous and ill-defined, and the fact that the bishop is involved through his licence does not help to solve practical problems on the spot. In the last analysis, the relationship is bound to be personal in character, and it is at this level that it can work or all too easily break down. An over-busy incumbent may be tempted to see his new recruit—and perhaps he can be excused in this—very largely in terms of the extra fillip and impetus he can bring to the life of the parish. The result is that he may, because of his curate's youth, tend to unload on him all the work among young people, forgetting that age is not the only criterion for suitability. A tired incumbent whose ways are set and rigid, and who has lost a little of the enthusiasm of some twenty years earlier, can be pardoned (though this does not make it right) an unconscious irritation with this new arrival, so naïvely optimistic that he will revolutionise the church within a twelve-month and that, if only he had full control, congregations would be astronomical; or, if they were not, the emptiness would be due to the offence of the Gospel! 'Bliss was it in that dawn to be alive, and to be young was very heaven.' The tragedy is that this optimism passes all too soon. As indeed it did with Wordsworth!

In a relationship which is in itself exposed to difficulty, everything depends, if the early years of training are to be of the greatest benefit, on the nature of the personal encounter involved. An ordinand, therefore, in seeking a title, though he ought not to be indifferent to the wholeness of the experience which a particular parish offers, is wise to go to a vicar who can be most helpful in these formative and extremely important years. They must be years of challenge, but they ought not to be years of agonising frustration. If they are so, it is usually because the relationship between the vicar and his curate is wrong. The fault can be on either side, usually both: but the incumbent, as the older and more experienced man, must accept the greater responsibility for a breakdown. With the present shortage of clergy to man the parishes, ordinands usually have no difficulty in fixing themselves up. Indeed, they are often in the position to indulge the luxury of a fairly wide choice. This ought to make possible a wise decision; but it can also lead to decisions made for the wrong reasons. One thing is quite certain. An unhappy first curacy is a thoroughly bad and unsatisfactory introduction to the ministry and can lead to a great deal of subsequent disillusionment. Clashes of temperament and mutual lack of understanding easily prove both destructive and disastrous, leading to wastage and strain all round. Their effects in a community cannot be confined to the two persons immediately involved.

There is no one answer to a practical problem of this kind and too many manuals fail to take account of the rich diversity in human nature which means in effect that what may be a useful discipline for one man can be a paralysing restriction to another. I remember an old man confessing to me that as a curate he sighed with relief when he heard his vicar taking his boots off in the bedroom of the clergy house above him. At last there was peace. Perhaps there is room for this kind of spartan severity, for unremitting labour and a rigid discipline: but this is not suitable for every man. Excessive challenge can break, as too feeble a challenge can debilitate. What Toynbee asserts of the growth of civilisations is equally true in the development of persons. There must be the right degree of stimulus for growth, neither too much nor too little. This means that an assistant curate ought to be left sufficiently free to develop along the lines of his God-given particularity; and a wise vicar will both recognise and foster this development. He will know that what begins in the younger man as a genuine self-expression can degenerate into a somewhat wilful assertion. Yet he may see even the latter as potentially the creative travail of a person reaching out to be himself. Perhaps it is the sin against the Holy Ghost to try to quench the eager questing of the young: to pour cold water on the belief that rebel human nature can tomorrow be tamed if only the right word is spoken and appropriate action taken. This optimism will disappear all too soon and often in its wake there comes a far more dangerous condition—a pessimism that ceases to believe in the unexpected, which refuses to hope for the dynamic victory of the good, which despairs of the breaking through of God's Kingdom.

A practical difficulty for many an assistant curate in his first parish is where to live. (His income is usually about £550 per annum, though it varies from diocese to diocese and equally from parish to parish.) Some clergy-houses are delightful, usually where they include laymen. Such an environment can provide a stimulating extension of student days, frank and free companionship, with the occasional excitement of hearing the bells ring at midnight. Institutions of this kind, however, can be dull, dreary and grim, a veritable weariness to the flesh. To live with the vicar is not as a rule ideal though to every rule there are exceptions. 'Digs' in the parish can also present problems. The too devoted landlady is not an unmixed blessing—indeed she can be a positive menace, for excessive deference to a young priest may encourage a false sense of importance and go a long way to produce a somewhat disagreeable person. The 'digs' which never offer privacy can also prove intolerable—but, of course, there is occasionally the absolutely right landlady. She is more precious than rubies!

Perhaps it might be added here that a very real difficulty for some clergy, though a new social situation has made it far less obtrusive, is the fact that during the day so much of their work and personal relations are set within a predominantly female community. This environmental situation must be recognised in order that its possible psychological effects can be offset. That they are very real in some men is only too obvious and it is within this context, at the beginning of a young curate's ministry, that the too obsequious landlady must be placed.

In some respects in this matter of accommodation the married priest has the advantage. There is something exciting in a young husband and wife entering together into this new experience—provided of course she is the right kind of wife for this particular person, and *vice versa*. Marriage during a first curacy is not perhaps to be advised. It is better either to go to the parish married, or to defer marriage to a more convenient season—that is, till the next curacy comes along. But here again a general rule does not always apply.

For the new assistant curate his most difficult problem is psychological, though he may not himself be aware of it. The sudden change in his life will probably prove a difficult period of transition, bringing with it a sense of loneliness. He will find that people's reactions to him (rightly or wrongly) have subtly changed, and he will not be experienced enough to counter this by a personal response capable of breaking through the unreality. He will (if he is a young man) miss the camaraderie of college with its more direct and uninhibited personal relations, and he will not immediately sense the pulse of the parochial community, even where it is beating strongly. He will also know, deep down within himself, that he is inadequate to deal with many of the personal problems that are brought to him: and he will soon discover how different is the 'face to face' meeting with people from the more tidy case-book examples, with their happy endings, too often given him in his lectures on pastoralia. His inward sense of need may encourage him to parade a confidence he does not feel and to conceal his insecurity under the mask of authority.

A wise vicar will recognise this personal situation for what it is. He has been through it himself.

Sometimes the position of the young curate is easier when he is one of a team of clergy; but such teams of clergy are comparatively rare, and are, anyhow, not necessarily most helpful for every man.

(2) INCUMBENT

We now turn to consider the assistant curate who after one or two curacies spread over a period of some six or seven years——this period is shorter now than it used to be—himself becomes a rector or vicar, placed in charge of a parish. By what means is this brought about?

The immediate and simple answer is that he has been 'offered' a living and has chosen to accept it. True his bishop may have suggested that he ought to go there, and the patron may have urged acceptance of the nomination, but he remains perfectly free to say 'Yes' or 'No'. There is, in the Church of England no direction at present, from authority comparable to that which exists, for example, in the Church of Rome, whereby a particular man of necessity accepts a given responsibility. (I am excluding here, of course, members of religious orders inside the Church of England.)* That he *ought* to accept a living offered him may be put very strongly to him but finally he must, under God, make up his own mind and accept full resonsibility for his decision. When he goes to his parish it is not under compulsion. In this respect the Church of England expects (and encourages) its clergy to act responsibly and for the right reasons.

There are, of course, advantages and disadvantages in such a way of doing things: but as suggested earlier in another context no system can combine every possible 'good'. Certainly freedom of choice does make great demands on a man's integrity and strength of will: and it can impose on him, in respect of his own family, agonising conflicts of loyalty. The natural man—and there is a great deal of the natural man in all of us—often finds it hard to make the right choice against his own inclinations: and this can have serious consequences at a time when the available manpower in the church is emphatically not distributed to the best advantage throughout the length and breadth of the country—or indeed throughout parts of the world where the Anglican church has responsibilities. In making his decision,

* See p. 147.

a priest is not always aware of these wider parochial and world situations within which his personal choice ought to be made. But this does not mean that authoritarian direction is necessarily the right answer, though if certain reforms to the parochial set-up are to be undertaken it is difficult to see how some of them can be effected without some such expedient. This, however, is not quite the same problem.

There is certainly value in the principle of free consent, and to whittle it away might subtly change the character of the Church of England clergy—and not necessarily for the better. What would seem to be important is that the facts relating to the present distribution of clergy should be made more widely known, thus revealing where the courageous and enterprising man is most needed. It is always better to secure an end by evoking a response to challenge rather than by a simple coercion. There is no reason to despair of the former being successful. Indeed there ought always to be a challenge involved in the vocation to the priesthood and more emphasis placed on a call to sacrifice. This is the best way, in the long run, to get the best men.

Yet a community which seeks to be Christ-committed must finally stand for a personal order, built upon a deep respect for the integrity of people; and this means, usually, that a particular ministry is better undertaken when it is undertaken freely. This is not to affirm for a single moment that there is no place in the Church of England for clergy in religious orders, unmarried and vowed in every respect to obedience. There certainly is. What it does imply, however, is that by and large a particular ministry is best discharged when entered upon as a matter of personal decision.

The criteria which a man takes account of (or ought to) in accepting the offer of a living will be many and various. Guidance from the Spirit does not operate in a vacuum. Essential in the weighing up of pros and cons is the honest facing up to the question as to whether his particular gifts will be best used in *this* community; whether he has the sheer physical energy to meet the demands which it must make upon him; whether for him an industrial or non-industrial, a sub-

urban, a town, or a country parish seems to offer the environment in which he feels he can make his best contribution. Some
men are temperamentally more suited to the country: others,
like Dr. Johnson and St. Paul, to the busy streets of a great city.
Here (for self-knowledge is not easily come by, though one
acquires a little more as one grows older) a frank talk with a
candid friend, who knows him well, will doubtless prove helpful.
Later in his ministry a man may feel a desperate need to change
the type of parish from that in which he has worked hitherto.
Over-specialisation is not always a good thing and such a change
may well prove a real refreshment and provide much needed
stimulus.

In making his decision it must be recognised that the married
man will have to consider his family. At certain periods in his
life he is not so mobile as his unmarried brother, and the wishes
of a wife, concerned for her children, cannot, and ought not
to be ignored. For better or for worse they are in this thing
together. Such considerations may seem to introduce a self-
regarding yardstick hardly in keeping with the sacrificial
demands of the Kingdom. Such a judgment, however, is
somewhat superficial.

The Church of England clergy, since the Reformation, have
been allowed to marry, and this has greatly enriched the
parochial ministry. Such married men have certain specific
advantages when it is a matter of discharging a resident cure.
But this does mean that the married man cannot ignore the
claims of his family when he is deciding where he is to serve,
though this will not for a moment imply that he is thereby
freed from a sacrificial decision. His family are involved with
him in his work—and their attitudes are bound to affect him,
and their reactions overflow into the life of the parish. It would
not be right, for example, for a man to go to a smoke-laden
industrial parish if his wife were in process of recovering from
tuberculosis and this might really prejudice her restoration to
full health. I mention such a crude example, simply to illustrate
in bolder relief the general principle that I have in mind. To do
the right thing for his family is what the vicar would expect of
his parishioners, and he would think less of them if they did not

respect this loyalty. It is important, therefore, that he should be prepared to do so himself. The *right* decision, of course, is no less demanding because concern for his immediate family is involved in it; for a priest and wife worthy of their salt will find excitement and stimulus in responding to a challenge. But a man who rides rough-shod over the legitimate needs of his family is not really witnessing to a personal order: nor will his ministry be sensitively directed towards particular people themselves often caught up in similar situations. To be aware of his own family is part of his witness to building the Kingdom: it does not represent a falling away from loyalty, but rather seeing the whole of life in its total commitment as integrally bound up with such a priority. Only when they see this put into practice will parishioners really be helped. The best and most mature priests (and wives!) usually reconcile both loyalties to the mutual advantage of each of them.

In saying this, I am not, of course, urging for a single moment that clergy should think in terms of financial rewards or prospects: but that a married man needs to see his responsibilities to his own family as part of his dedication and witness to the the Kingdom of God.

An obvious lesson to be learnt from such considerations (and I have already referred to it) is the undoubted need for unmarried priests, working alongside the married. Both have their parts to play and each has advantages peculiar to his estate. The Church of England would be the poorer if one kind existed in isolation, though I myself would always hope for a majority of married men in the parochial ministry—and it is this ministry that I am discussing at the moment. Yet it remains true that the unmarried man has greater mobility, and can make himself more easily available for emergency situations and *ad hoc* needs. He has no family to move and his financial position is less complicated. The same is, of course, equally true of the members of a religious community.

But to return. An incumbent takes up his ministry in the parish as a result of his own desire to go there. This is a good beginning; and it offers him an initial advantage with his

parishioners. To be introduced into such a relationship of trust
with them is a great privilege, and it is understandable if
parishioners think that there is no parish quite like their own.
In certain respects they are absolutely right, and a sensitive
vicar soon becomes vividly aware of the individuality of his own
community—its unique traditions and history, if it has one! A
parish is not necessarily more important because its population
is larger, more intelligent, more wealthy; or because its church
is more beautiful or the income of the living higher. Some of the
most distinguished parochial ministries in the Church of
England—perhaps the most distinguished have never been
heard of at all in the wider world—have been discharged in
remote villages, off the beaten track, or in the wretched slums
of great industrial cities. One thinks of Charles Kingsley at
Eversley, Fletcher at Madeley, Grimshaw at Haworth, Keble at
Hursley, Wainwright at St. Alban's, Holborn. A relatively small
parish (provided it is not too small) offers the compensatory
possibility of really getting to know people well, and people
usually become the more interesting the more intimate the
relationship. 'I have known X drunk and I have known him
sober; but there is nothing in him'—this is an amusing jest but
in the nature of the case terribly superficial when said of any
man. Nor do people become more important in themselves
because they are V.I.P.s. It was Archbishop Lang's pathetic
mistake—what a colourful and dramatic person he was!—to
think that they did, though fortunately he could laugh at himself (sometimes) particularly at his 'snob's progress' into the
north of England, to quote his own vivid description. Yet
V.I.P.s *are* important (as is everyone else) and it is an inverted
form of snobbery to write them off—though candour compels the confession that the temptation to do so is somewhat
rare!

The incumbent chooses to go to his parish: but how does
the offer, or invitation, come to him? The answer again is
simple. He is nominated by a patron, and the patron may be
the Crown, the bishop of the diocese, a cathedral or collegiate
church, the incumbent of a parish, a college, a private trust or
a single person. This may seem a very odd procedure for it

certainly suggests a lack of system and great untidiness. It is untidy: and it is so as the result of a long and complex history. Nobody ever decided around a table that this was the best way of nominating the right person to the appropriate living. Private patronage, as it is called, goes back to very distant days, even before the Norman Conquest, when the local lord built the church and maintained the parson. In the case of Westminster Abbey, for example, which has some twenty-six livings in its gift, this represents the legacy of the vast estates which it owned all over the country before such expedients as the Westminster Abbey Appeal were ever thought of. Now all that remains is the patronage of the livings, though it is an 'all' which can be rich in contemporary significance.

The right question to ask, however, is not whether the system is untidy—life is very untidy—but whether, if it is not wrong in principle, it works well: and whether, moreover, there is a reasonable presumption that it works better, that is, does what it is required to do more effectively, than any other system which might be devised. Such questions are, perhaps, unanswerable in any absolute sense because it is self-evident that a non-existing system or way of doing things can hardly be appraised except by comparison with some other church which works things this way. In a matter of this kind it will suffice, in this book at least, if I suggest some of its advantages and disadvantages.

There is certainly a potential value in a wide spread of patronage. It ensures that a variety of interests are involved and given responsibility, and this in a way that would not so easily be secured if all such patronage were in the hands of the bishop of the diocese or even, which would be better, in an electoral college (though such a college could go some way to bringing this about). The present procedure associates great institutions and corporate societies with the well-being of the Church of England: and thereby helps to prevent theological intolerance and inbreeding. It avoids a concentration of power in a few hands; and secures an effective lay influence, thus preventing excessive clerical control. It leads to a large variety of type in the parochial ministry and prevents the emergence of one kind of fashionable parson. In particular the party trust, though open to grave abuse, does help to preserve a diverse tradition within the Church of England.

As a by-product, this way of doing things encourages a healthy independence among the clergy, and its non-official character prevents ecclesiastical introversion, for it roots the church in the many-sided life of the nation. The rebel and the man who is 'agin authority' is more likely to be given responsibility this way. In particular, such a method offsets the temptation to offer a man a particular living because of his seniority or by reason of the fact that he has in the past served the diocese well. The private patron can, in the nature of the case, have no interest but to secure the most suitable incumbent for his living. This is his strength though on occasions, because of the limitation involved, it can also prove his weakness. Yet the fact that he is somewhat detached from the ecclesiastical scene may add up to his making an independent judgment. It is not unfair to suggest of many patrons, that nice ecclesiastical and theological distinctions fly over their heads; but this is not always a handicap when deciding the best pastor for a given parish. Lay prejudice, on the other hand ('give us a man who doesn't meddle in politics') can be a very real danger. I know of a private patron who insisted that his nominee should have served in the army, preferably in the Guards!

Certainly to concentrate patronage in the hands of a diocesan bishop would make more difficult the right kind of relationship between him and his clergy. Nor would it always be easy for him to secure the right appointment even when he knew where to go for it—a fact to which the acute Dr. Hensley Henson, sometime Bishop of Durham, drew attention. The tendency would be for the bishop to appoint from within his own diocese because certain people had claims upon him, whereas it is important to avoid this kind of restriction. Moreover, as suggested earlier, a man of ability and prophetic gifts may have browsed in the perilous fields of unorthodoxy and it would therefore be difficult for ecclesiastical authority (and may be quite properly) to prefer him, since such authority is more deeply entrenched in the structure and traditions of the church as such. This could apply equally to official electoral colleges. The private patron, in a situation of this kind, can be irresponsibly responsible. He does not commit the church as a whole in the same way.

If there is some force in the above argument, then this makes it even more important that a number of livings should be at the disposal of the bishop of the diocese and for reasons which must have already become apparent. He is uniquely equipped to see, in a wide context, the diocesan situation: and it is of overriding importance that parishes should not be regarded as unrelated, atomistic units, but themselves part of an organic whole. His wider view is a wholesome corrective: he stands for a larger 'cell' within the living body of the church of Christ. Particularly is this the case where local prejudice needs to be overcome and tiny villages brought together.

We must not forget, however, the criticisms, and they are serious ones, which can be directed against the system as it operates at present.

Some private patrons are shockingly slack and irresponsible, discharging their duties in a perfunctory manner: in which case it is better if they pass the matter over to the bishop, that is, of course, if they cannot be persuaded to act responsibly. But such is true of a relatively small number, and the solution is not necessarily to abolish the private patron altogether. Many of them take infinite pains. But the existence of so many private interests can make it difficult for a man to go to another parish when he thinks he needs a change. More serious, however, is it that the present system, by perpetuating so many independent rights, and identifying a parish with the existence of a church, makes far more difficult a radical reappraisal of the present parochial set-up and the deployment of the clergy. It prevents an 'over-all' look, and can encourage the wrong kind of parochialism, with the clinging to sectional interests when they have become a sheer anachronism. It is reckoned at the present moment that some 41·7 per cent of the clergy minister to some 11·2 per cent of the population, while at the other end of the scale 14·6 per cent minister to 34·7 per cent. The implication of such figures would seem to be plain, though perhaps not quite so plain as a too superficial or hasty judgment might suggest.

A final word. No-one starting *de novo* would dream of instituting a system of patronage such as that which at present obtains, and there are undoubted defects in it. As already suggested the existence of so many built-in and separate rights could constitute a hindrance to a drastic resettlement. Yet, there is, I believe, great value, in a broad context, in the present way of doing things. That it should exist at all is due to a past history: to a civilising church generating a people, thereby rooting itself within its social structures. In so far as such a pattern has a presupposition (even if a concealed one) it is that the church is inevitably and deeply involved in the life of the nation, and that what happens in either of them is of concern to both. If the untidy logic of such a system should at any time prove in practice a disservice to the primary task for which the church exists, namely to build the Kingdom of Christ; or if the state itself should wish the relationship to cease, then it must go. This is a contemporary debate which lies outside the scope of this book: but it may be hoped that if a new way of doing things emerges it will not lose the undoubted values of the old.

As to the patron, it is important to add that once he has appointed to a living, his responsibility ceases, except that his consent is necessary, for example, in the case of alterations to the parsonage house or the sale of glebe. He cannot interfere with the incumbent in the latter's discharge of his duty or the day-to-day running of the parish.

So far we have been concerned with the patron and his nominee: but what of the parishioners who are at the receiving end? Have they any say in this matter which affects them so intimately? The question is important particularly since the suggestion has been made that the local clergy should be drawn from those who have already distinguished themselves as natural lay leaders of the Christian community around them.

Until fairly recent times, it must be admitted that parishioners had no say. Unless some definite complaint, such as immorality or heretical opinion was sustained against the patron's nominee, the parish had of necessity to accept whoever was sent to it. For centuries this was not considered a hardship: rather it was regarded as given in the nature of things, in the same way as weather has to be accepted good or more usually bad. (It is worth noting, however, that a few parishes, St. Peter Mancroft in Norwich for example, established the right of nominating the incumbent through their vestry, and still retain this right to-day.) The Church of England was not thought of as a democratic institution. Bishops were not elected by the voice of the people and it would never have occurred to Englishmen that they ought to elect their parish priest. Perhaps they were right, for election in a matter of this kind is certainly not always wise, particularly since the criteria for office are by no means self-evident and collective judgments are often both ill-informed and superficial. The case for democracy is not necessarily that it leads to the right decision, but that it makes people responsible for the decision that they have made and thereby encourages them to make it work. But the incumbent is not and ought not to be responsible to his parishioners in this kind of way, though he has a great responsibility for them.

Parishioners to-day, however, have certain rights in the appointment of their incumbent if they care to use them. Since the Benefices Exercise of Rights of Presentation Measure, 1931, a procedure has been set up by which the bishop of the diocese, when a benefice is to become vacant, must notify the patron and the parochial church council. The council may then, if it wishes, and it must do this within thirty days, make representations to the patron in writing of the conditions, needs, and the traditions of the parish and the kind of man which it regards as suitable. It must not, however, mention any particular name. A copy of such representation must be sent to the bishop. If there should later be a stalemate arising from the unwillingness of the churchwardens, acting on behalf of the council, to accept the patron's nominee, then the bishop is required to refer the matter to a body of advisors.

It is not, I think, naïvely optimistic to claim that on the whole this *via media*, or rather this endeavour to combine the best of both worlds, seems to work fairly well. If the parish itself were to elect or nominate, its choice in practice would be from a very limited 'clientele'. Former curates would undoubtedly return in abundance to their old parishes, only to find (I suspect) that there is all the difference in the world between being an assistant curate and having final responsibility. P.C.C.s cannot be blamed because they decide that the evil they know is to be preferred to the evil that they 'wot not of'! This, however, is a counsel of prudential fear: and the security of 'I've grown accustomed to his face' is not always to be sought after. Also, as we know from the political sphere, the man who secures office through election—and on the whole this seems to work best in politics—often has his hands tied in advance. There are pledges to redeem.

On the other hand, to ignore local feeling and to seem to be indifferent to needs and conditions on the spot, especially as it is always helpful for the new incumbent to be able to count on an initial good-will, does not seem to be either wise or right. In practice, it must be admitted, a particular name is often communicated unofficially by the churchwardens to the patron, but the latter is under no obligation whatever to accept it, if he is not, in conscience, convinced that the person so named is best suited to the parish.

After the patron's nominee has been accepted by the parochial church council, the incumbent elect is introduced into his living at a special service in the parish church. On this occasion he is 'instituted' into a cure of souls, that is, given spiritual and pastoral responsibility for his parishioners by the bishop who says: 'Accept this charge, yours and mine.' He is also 'inducted' by the archdeacon into possession of the church and benefice, with the emoluments of his office.

The latter ceremony is interesting and colourful. It begins with the archdeacon escorting the parish priest outside the church and placing his hand upon the key or ring of the door while he pronounces the words of induction. The door is then opened and the incumbent tolls the bell, after which the mandate is returned to the bishop, the certificate of induction being endorsed. The priest attended by the churchwardens is then escorted to the font, the prayer desk, the lectern, the pulpit and the communion table, at all of which prayers for his ministry are offered.

The order of such a service of institution and induction, even if it is somewhat archaic and legal in form, can yet be made most impressive. Recent additions, associating parishioners with the incumbent in a common responsibility, have undoubtedly added to its vitality and relevance. Certainly it is an occasion which has great significance in the life of a parish—another chapter in its continuing history.

Instituted and inducted into his living, the patron's nominee now becomes the *persona** or parson of the parish. He is usually known as either rector or vicar, a distinction which has now ceased to have any particular meaning and need not, therefore, detain us. It will be necessary, in succeeding chapters, to consider what his essential task is, but before doing this one more question ought to be asked. It is an important one.

How long after his institution and induction does he stay in the parish as its incumbent? The answer legally is, until he resigns to his bishop or dies—provided, that is, he commits no offence, nor suffers a disability, such as to lead to his deprivation.† A 'clerk in holy orders' in the Church of England, when he goes to his parish, is inducted into a freehold, and as is well known, freeholds are zealously guarded by the law of the land and no arbitrary invasion of their rights is tolerated. Here there is a difference from the system which obtains for ministers in the Free Churches, where, generally, no such life security exists.

In the last century, and earlier, it was by no means exceptional for a young man to go to a first living and to remain there for the rest of his life. He (though not always, I suspect, his parishioners!) saw no reason why he should remove himself elsewhere. Mercifully relieved from any ecclesiastical ambition, and bringing up his large family in the rectory, the tendency

* In medieval England the *persona* (in M.E. *persone*) was a 'rector of a parish' and as such could then be a layman. Its popular use, however, was later extended to include 'a vicar, or any beneficed clergyman, a chaplain, a curate, any clergyman'.

† This does not apply to some fifteen Guild Churches established in the City of London, where appointment is for a term of years.

was for him to stay put. Such long incumbencies are most exceptional these days: and indeed many feel (myself included) care will have to be taken to ensure that the pendulum does not swing to the other extreme. To-day the average length statistically seems to be between ten and eleven years.*

It is obvious, of course, that in a delicate matter of this kind no hard and fast rules can easily be drawn up. There *is* something to be said for the moderately long incumbency, though this is by no means to say that all incumbencies ought to be long. People and parishes differ, and a man himself changes across the years. What can be said is that length of days does at least make possible the building up of personal relationships of mutual trust: it means that often the incumbent has time on his side—he can afford to wait and be patient. He can become a repository of local wisdom, an intimate friend of the family over one or even two generations. Such a status in a parish comes only when it is given time to grow; and this is particularly the case with the man whose personality is not immediately forthcoming, and who has a natural reserve or shyness.

Such considerations as the above, however, can become a little unreal unless the modern sociological situation is taken into account, for it might well be argued that in a rapidly changing contemporary scene, in which people are more mobile, here to-day and gone to-morrow, length of years does not add up as it used to do. There is some truth in this, though it could be said on the other side that the need to preserve both continuity and identity—which need the parish priest is in a unique position to meet—is even greater in a changing community.

The too long incumbency does, however, expose a man to particular difficulties. There are times when the best of parish priests is ripe for the stimulus of change, both for his own sake and for the sake of those to whom he ministers. Men grow stale and become played-out: and parishioners can get tired of the same face and mannerisms. Sometimes a priest has made his contribution and it is in the interests of everybody that he

* I doubt whether this figure represents a real average for a majority of incumbencies, though it may well be a correct statistical average.

should go elsewhere. It may also be that a man has not done well in a particular parish. He has made mistakes and since it is difficult for him to live them down he had better learn from past failure and cut loose. 'To-morrow to fresh woods and pastures new.' Sometimes a man does redeem himself in another parish.

As I have said so often, in a variety of contexts, matters of this kind cannot easily be reduced to precise law and order and it is often unwise to attempt to do so. Allowing for this, however, it can sometimes happen that the very fluidity of the Anglican system lays it open on occasions to grave abuses. Certainly in this respect, it imposes a very heavy burden on the conscience of the incumbent, because no matter what advice he may receive from trusted friends, from his family, from his bishop, his parishioners, finally the decision is his own; and it is doubtful whether a man in these particular circumstances is always the best judge and jury in his own cause. Indeed sometimes when we know perfectly well what we ought to do, it is difficult to translate good intention into right action, even though other people may be seriously injured if we decide wrongly. What is wanted is a system sufficiently determinate to ensure the elimination of gross abuses, yet sufficiently flexible to meet given situations. Maybe this is a counsel of perfection. The Anglican system can on occasions be gloriously right: and right where a too rigid pattern would be unable to contrive things so successfully. Yet at its least fortunate it can and does lead to shocking waste and misapplication of manpower with a consequent devitalising of the life of a parish for many years. Nowhere is this seen more vividly than in the matter of retirement, and it is here, probably, that something could be done.

The freehold, as it operates at the moment, means that there is no compulsory retiring age (though a man at seventy after a minimum of forty years' service is entitled to a pension of £400 per year). Can this situation really be justified? The sad fact is that the freehold, which most definitely has its advantages, gives protection to those who deserve it as well as to those who do not. It can encourage independence in that an Anglican parson is not at the mercy of his parishioners and this makes it the more easy, human nature being as it is, for him to champion right but unpopular causes and remain to see them through. It can and does provide security for the prophet—though security for him is not always an unmixed blessing. Yet the freehold can protect the inefficient as well as the efficient, the lazy as well as the hard working; it can make a man cosy, comfortable and complacent when he ought to be perpetually challenged and sometimes ill at ease.

True it is that the freehold has in part been broken in upon by recent legislation (the Incumbents Disability Measure, 1945: and the Ecclesiastical Jurisdiction Measure, 1964) which makes it possible to remove a parish priest on account of age and infirmity, or because of misconduct or gross neglect of duty. Yet the machinery is clumsy and resort to it usually leads to unhappy consequences, as a particular case some years ago made evident. But this measure does provide an extreme remedy for a very extreme situation. What would seem to be both right and fitting is that, in addition, when an incumbent reaches a certain age the decision as to whether he is to continue ought not to be left entirely in his own hands. This is neither fair to him nor to his parishioners, and it ought not to be difficult to devise a system to prevent a man being both judge and jury in his own case.

This does not mean, in my judgment, that the church needs to go along with the 'secular' world in the increasingly younger age at which men retire. This may be right in some professions because of the need to promote younger men, and perhaps to make it possible for the 'retiree' to use wisely and positively his latter years. It is more than doubtful whether quite the same criteria apply or ought to apply in respect of the priesthood. A man of sixty-five or seventy, though his physical energy and capacity to act under pressure have declined, may be in the full flood of his powers as a pastor. Experience can be invaluable where a personal ministry is to be discharged, for the 'know how' of a priest is not a matter of pure technical expertise. A hard and fast rule for retirement could lead either to wastage or indulgence: but to fix an age at which the decision to carry on is not left entirely in the interested person's own hands is quite another matter and is highly desirable. There ought to be

E

some impartial review and assessment. The parson in a parish is in a unique position and many will suffer, and the building of God's Kingdom be impaired, if he is obviously, through age, inadequate. As it is, of course, the decision is often determined by factors which are not really relevant to the parochial situation in itself; but very important in respect of the incumbent (i.e. financial considerations, accommodation, etc.).

If this matter of retirement, however, is to be tackled effectively at various levels, it is important that a new attitude to office should be born within the church: and that men should cease to see certain posts in terms of status and prestige. This may well mean that older men should be prepared to go where their more limited energies do not constitute so severe a handicap. A. W. Hopkinson of *Pastor's Progress* (a very fine parish priest) ended his life where he began—as an assistant curate. Indeed in former days there used to be many men who felt this to be their particular vocation and never held an independent cure.

There is always work which a retired priest, if he still has some energy and has retained his enthusiasm, can undertake. He can speak out of a rich experience acquired across the years.

Once again, in this matter of the freehold, there is the possibility of both good and evil. At its best it can stand for a relationship between priest and people which is not a kind of 'service tenancy', contractual in nature and terminable willy-nilly after a definite period of years. Human relations are not like this. Fidelity is of their essence, and there are situations (very rare it may be) when a developed Christian community might be asked and expected to 'carry' its pastor, bear with and perhaps recreate him.

It is certainly a matter for thankfulness that Pope John was not retired before he was raised to the pontificate. Age can have its peculiar merits.

On the other hand the freehold admits of the most severe abuses and can even serve to encourage in a priest a laziness and indifference which he himself, in his better moments, would deplore.

I am sure that there is a mean here between two extremes and that it is not beyond the wit of the Church of England to find it. The danger is a doctrinaire approach which applies a ruthless logic at the expense of sensitivity and insight.

The problem is to retain the values of the freehold—and it has considerable values—while at the same time scaling down its disvalues. To destroy it root and branch could inflict an irreparable loss.

CHAPTER 4

PRIEST AND PARISH

BEFORE dealing, in some detail, with the day-to-day work of the parish priest, it will be helpful briefly to concern ourselves with two themes. First with what he, as a Christian minister, is finally seeking to do; and secondly what it means to do this in a parish.

The parish priest is commissioned by the church to witness to and to build the Kingdom of Christ. This Kingdom is a personal order in which men, in free and mature relations with each other, give glory to God. If its full realisation is beyond this temporal world, it is here and now, in the actuality of given situations, in day-to-day living, that we begin to build it. Society is to become a family: men are to live together as brothers.

The supreme expression of this quality of personal living is seen, by the Christian, as existing throughout eternity within the Being of God, who in His absolute perfection shows how men are to be fulfilled in their relations with each other. In God (the language used here is, of course, highly analogical) the love of the Father eternally begets the Son, and this love returns through the Spirit back to the Father. Here is a 'society' in which there is no aggression of the one 'person' against the other. True there are distinctions, analogous to what we at the level of our human experience understand as distinctions between persons, but all is held together in the one community ('substantial ground') through an energising love.

Yet the Christian does not only glimpse an end, a pattern of living, which is perfectly realised in God. He further believes that Jesus, in this ordinary everyday world of ours, lived as already in that ordered kingdom, thereby showing how power is released to build it—the power which flows from God through sacrificial self-giving. Central to his whole ministry or life's work was this supreme dedication. He saw himself as inaugurating the Kingdom, the unique servant in whom the old prophetic hope was to be given a creative leap forward.

Every community, therefore every order of persons, whether it be a family, or indeed a factory, must move towards this divine 'economy' of persons if it is, through purposeful growth, to realise the potential of those who compose it. This means that men must overcome their inner frustration, their terrible feeling of disunity, estrangement and division, by ceasing to be assertive and aggressive against each other. They must find their true home in a society of persons: they must, as far as men can, live out the life of God in dedication to His will, and in right relations one with another. Commitment to Jesus is therefore no solitary or isolated act of loyalty, but leads to association with a community enterprise which continues his saving work.

The Christian, however, is not so simple as to imagine that this Kingdom can be established in the twinkling of an eye. Rebel human nature is not so easily made whole. A naïve perfectionism is no part of his Gospel: but he does believe that no matter how resistant the context—and it is often very resistant both in collective behaviour and in more intimate human relations—he must strive to lift human affairs into the higher dimension of a truly personal society in which alone men are fulfilled: and that as he does this he will receive power. It matters little what words we use to describe this process, whether it be redemption, transvaluation, integration, so long as we know what we are talking about and that what we say refers to a real and existing human situation. Men need not only the vision of what ought to be, but resources of power to incarnate the vision here and now. A ministry both of word and sacrament is necessary.

I hope I may be forgiven for what might seem a digression from my main theme. True this is not a book about theology as such, but I find it impossible to talk about the 'saving' work of the parish priest unless it is first placed within a wide context of man's total life. Theology is concerned with what God has done and is doing to make men whole. Whatever the immediate duties of the parish priest are, and they are often very immediate and seemingly pedestrian, his purpose through them is to be the servant by whom and in whom God builds His Kingdom. At the risk of seemingly wearisome repetition, I repeat that this is the overriding purpose of the church of Christ in whatever century and wherever established. How it sets about this task will vary with the particular situation in which it finds itself in time, place and circumstance: but what it is finally seeking to do does not vary.

The priest goes to his parish as an ordained minister of the Church of God commissioned to serve in the Church of England. One thing is quite certain, and it must be said even if it appears somewhat preciously pious. Unless the Kingdom is being built in him, unless he is in himself excitingly alive, exploring in depth the experience which entry into the Kingdom brings along with it, then he and his ministry will lack power and lose direction. Of course God will providentially work through him, for people are often used in spite of themselves: but he could be used to more purpose when there is a free and co-operative response. And such a response means that he himself is always in a process of becoming. No one expects him to have fully arrived.

From this glimpse of the end, we now come down to earth to consider the particular territory, the local scene in which the parish priest is to work. John Wesley used to say of himself that the world was his parish, and that same world may well be grateful that he took so cosmic a view of his responsibilities. His work for the Kingdom was mammoth in its achievement. But we are not all John Wesleys and the call of the parish priest is not usually so extensive. He is entrusted with a cure of souls by the bishop within a particular neighbourhood. This means in the best sense of the term—though emphatically not in its pejorative use—that he must be parochially minded. This need not be a limitation. The parish is part of a diocese, the diocese of a province, the province of a communion and the communion of a universal church, the congregation of Christian people dispersed throughout the whole world. The introverted, sel-

regarding parish (i.e. local community) does not make sense nor does it, moreover, express what the Kingdom is like. It is equally true, however, that larger loyalties spring out of lesser: that a man is more likely to love other people's countries if he begins by loving his own. Benjamin Disraeli was right (he was not always right by any means!) when he poured scorn on 'cosmopolitan critics, friends of every country but their own'. Jean-Jacques Rousseau—what an extraordinarily arresting creature he was—is said to have been a great lover of humanity but an equally great despiser of men. This is the wrong way round. Certainly he never found it easy to enter into fulfilled relations with particular people.

The first responsibility of the parish priest, then, is to begin to build the Kingdom of Christ in the place where he is, remembering always that the parish is part of a wider world, and if it is inward looking it will bog people down where they are, rather than release them. To discharge this first duty effectively means for the priest a concentrated attention directed towards his own people. He has a defined personal charge within a geographical territory, for every inch of English soil is situated within an ecclesiastical parish—the legacy of the church's long history of involvement. As we have seen, when the Anglo-Saxons came over from Europe, they preferred to settle in small communities in the countryside rather than occupy the Roman towns, and these communities and the land around them became the parish. The medieval legalists converted this piecemeal process into a tidy system.

Up to the time of the Reformation there was only one church and its authority was paramount. To-day, of course, this is no longer the case, with the result that among parishioners, in addition to members of the Church of England and those who make no religious profession, there may well be Roman Catholics, Free Churchmen, Quakers, Jews and other groups. This can have the effect of adding to the vitality of a Christian witness, provided, of course, that right and co-operative relationships exist between them. But historically (whatever be their theological view) these non-Anglican bodies represent gathered communities. The Church of England parson, on the other hand, when he is instituted into his parish, has entrusted to him a pastoral care over all those who live and work geographically within its boundaries. This is true whatever be their religious loyalty, or even if they are entirely without one. He is there to serve them all, impossible though this may be of achievement in a large and densely populated area. It would be quite improper for a Church of England parson to say to any parishioner who came to him for help: 'You are not a member of my congregation.' As the minister of an Established Church he accepts a definite responsibility for all those who reside in the parish entrusted to him. Or to put this round the other way, his parishioners—and mere physical residence confers such a status in this broad context—have a right to, and a claim upon, his ministrations. They can seek his help or advice at any time. Of course, and I shall say more about this later, such a position of responsibility imposes a heavy, sometimes it might seem an almost impossible, burden upon him, both in respect of time and nervous energy. True also that his help will continue to be sought only if he is the kind of person who can measure up to giving it: but this does not alter the basic fact that his position *vis-à-vis* his parishioners is as simple as this. He is placed where he is, by the Church of England through the person of the bishop, to exercise a pastoral care over all his people, churchgoer and non-church-goer, Christian and non-Christian, good and bad, old and young. This means that, on his part, he will feel free when visiting to knock on any door, as parishioners on their part will feel free to receive or not to receive him. The surprising thing—or is it so surprising?—is that he usually meets with great cordiality. I shall say more subsequently about such visiting: my point here is simply that an incumbent does not regard himself as concerned only with the members of his own congregation. In fact he accepts the widest possible responsibility and the psychology that prompts him to do this has been built up over the centuries.

It is because of this situation, that the Church of England has always tried to insist on the residence of its parochial clergy, that is, that they make their home on their cure. In the nature of the case they are not commuters. Indeed the whole parochial system, historically, has been geared to this requirement, though it has not always been easy to insist upon in practice. In the eighteenth century, for example, there was considerable non-residence*—it was probably not so great as sometimes supposed since absentee incumbents often saw to it that there was an assistant curate on the spot—due sometimes to the fact that there was neither parsonage house nor income, and some rural parishes were minute in size. Candour compels the admission, however, that there was a great deal of slackness and sheer incompetence. Yet at every visitation the bishop reiterated the question as to whether the parson was resident and if not why not.

To-day, and I shall return to this theme in respect of group ministries,† the incumbent does not always physically reside in what is technically his cure: but essentially the whole Anglican system is geared, and in my judgment rightly and necessarily geared, to residence.

The reasons why this requirement is essential, even if the precise form of it on occasions needs some adaptation, are overwhelming, though some of them are subtle in character. To be living in the midst of his people, and thus to be immediately accessible; to see every morning the same skyline, and to grumble at the same weather; for his wife to shop at the same stores; to be caught up and involved in the same local events and day-to-day life—these all create, and will continue to create a bond which is none the less real because it is difficult to define. It is true, of course, that often the integrity of the local community has been broken in upon. The young are taken out of it for their education. Many commute to work and enter into group loyalties not geographically contained within the parish itself. Yet this may make it more important than ever that there should be one person whose focal point is in the local community; who stands essentially for its continuing life; and who both resides and works where his parishioners are established with their families, even if they go out of it. When all is said and done, though a man may be many hours removed, and

* This was equally the case in the Middle Ages.
† See p. 76.

many miles away from his home during the day, it is still around his home that his most elemental emotions cluster.

The fact that so many people are rootless in these days suggests that there is a need, in a changed social and technological environment, for group loyalties to be brought together, unified and directed in the person who enters into them. A house divided against itself will fall, and it does not necessarily mean for a moment that the advent of a new social situation implies that in accepting it we are impotent to do anything about it. Within the new emerging pattern of rapid mobility and change, an increasing restlessness may well go along with it. The parish priest because of his unique status is in a unique position to do something about this—once again if he is big enough to measure up to the problem and opportunity. Of course, essential to his final theological position is his commitment to change, to the process of building a city, to men being *in via*, on a journey. Yet at the same time he stands for a city that has firm foundations, for the permanence of things and the final worth of persons. To accept that a man's home, because he goes out from it, is nothing but a dormitory and in the nature of the case can be nothing else, is to sell the pass and to invite personal catastrophe. The parish priest can help to make residence meaningful for himself and for others. That he should be seen walking about his parish* (not commuting from afar) contributes to making a natural meeting possible. This only happens from simply 'being around', and, let us be frank, from being willing on occasions to seem to waste time. And for the vicar to be bringing up his own family in the parish over which he has a pastoral care adds greatly to the personal character of his own ministry and the kind of community that he (with others) is seeking to build.

In this respect (though I would not wish to exaggerate in such a matter and for obvious reasons) there is a difference between the work of a doctor and that of a parish priest. The former is called in to deal with a specific ill, though in order to do this effectively he may well wish to become a friend of the family. The latter, however, has an overriding concern for the

* There are occasions when it is wise to abandon the car!

whole man all the time, 'in sickness and in health' and in the widest possible context. He is anxious to enter into effective personal relations and it is for this purpose that residence is important.

It needs to be added that it is, of course, wholly admirable that there are clergy in city churches who provide a ministry during the week for those in their parishes engaged in industry and commerce. The possibilities for pastoral work in the lunch-hour and for making contact with the personnel of great business houses are immense. Such a ministry is a realistic recognition of a contemporary situation.

Essential to residence is the vicarage or rectory—the parsonage house. Unlike the canon of a cathedral who may only be required to reside for some three months in the year, an incumbent is bound to live in his parsonage, unless he has an episcopal licence dispensing him, given only in exceptional circumstances. Essentially the vicarage is a private house, not a plant or an office, though the incumbent is usually relieved of rent and rates, and in most cases of dilapidations or upkeep. It may well be, particularly in the more populous parishes, or where the vicarage is too small, that the incumbent may at times find it necessary to work from some neutral or more official base: and indeed there are a few occasions, which need not be enumerated, when this is a wise thing to do; but such a method of work is no alternative to keeping an open house. The parish priest stands for, and himself tries to embody, a personal order, and this means establishing right relations between unique people. Here his wife is significant. She is not an unpaid curate, and unless she has particular gifts, or the need is absolutely desperate, she is wise to avoid running innumerable parochial organisations herself. If she does, she may well become over-tired, get involved with parishioners in the wrong way, and simply prevent other people exercising leadership. Also when she leaves the parish, a very real problem may be created if her successor cannot fit into the same pattern. Of course it is a good thing, when she has an interest of her own, to keep it up, and to make her contribution in her own way. For her to co-operate in welcoming parishioners into her home of itself helps to create a more intimate relationship. This makes it important that there exists between husband and wife a relationship which realises itself in the making of a household in which other people can feel at ease. If this is not the case, the incumbent's pastoral ministry will be made so much the more difficult and in extreme situations impossible.

The parsonage house has an important rôle to discharge in the total commitment of a pastor, and it is for this reason that the building of so many poky and inadequate vicarages up and down the country is to be deplored. Often they are not large enough for a family man and certainly lack the space (often the graciousness) needed for the particular function which they are called upon to discharge. It is certainly true that a large vicarage can be daunting, particularly to a wife who lacks imagination or is not physically fit, and nothing looks worse than a garden which has become a wilderness: but to get rid of such buildings with the haste characteristic of the moment may well prove to be a monumental folly.* The most elaborate plant, necessary as it often is, is no alternative to the intimacy of a parsonage house—and for this reason such a house needs to be large enough for the many uses to which the parish priest might wish to put it. He needs to be able to spread himself.

I have stressed as essential to his ministry the residence of the parish priest: but such residence need not always be conceived in too doctrinaire a manner. Many rural communities, though they have their own ancient church, are not large enough to constitute a real community, nor can they properly deploy the energies of a full-time priest. For every such parish to have its own parson would not only be wasteful of a limited personnel but could impose a frustrating isolation on many clergy, leading to a crippling sense of loneliness. It is for this reason that in a few parts of the country small parishes have been grouped together and are served from a centre by a team of clergy. The advantages of the 'system' (there are some disadvantages) are that it makes it possible for small villages to be more effectively catered for and for the villagers to enter into a richer com-

* I am assuming, of course, that they can be modernised—as is usually the case.

munity life sponsored by the church. For example, a group youth club can be established, and transport to it 'laid on'. The small village congregation can on occasions be swelled from other parishes equally small. A village choir becomes a possibility.

The group ministry certainly has much to commend it, particularly since, as children are often taken out of their village for education and adults to work, the small community is already conditioned to look outwards. Social structures change in response to new economic and technological needs. The mistake, of course, is to be doctrinaire in matters of this kind, and to assume that the group ministry is the answer to every problem in the countryside and elsewhere—the one normative way of doing things. It is not; though, judged practically, the results of the experiment so far seem to be encouraging. Some small communities have never had a resident parson, though this is not to say that no small community ought ever to have one. A man heavily committed in some other employment, like the Anglo-Saxon priest on his land, might be found to fit the bill. What is needed is a practical approach, freedom to experiment, and great manoeuvrability. I know, for example, a priest who has integrated his rural parish with a school to the great advantage of both. Only an exceptional person, maybe, has the ability and flair to do this. Perhaps the Church of England ministry needs more exceptional and imaginative men. The opportunities are there and they are immense.

The group ministry can also help to overcome the extreme loneliness which isolation sometimes brings to the priest in the remote village. His situation in this respect is quite different from that of his predecessor a century ago. In those days the country rectory housed a self-contained community and the incumbent enjoyed all the psychological security of a class structured society into which he entered at an understood level. To-day all too easily the parish priest can feel a homeless man, not quite knowing where he belongs. There are still about eight thousand single-handed incumbents. Yet it needs to be added that sometimes the fact that a parson is on his own means that he is forced to root himself, and find his friends, in the local community which he serves. Teams of clergy are not always an unmixed blessing: they can have the effect of re-moving the priest from laymen, and thus make for clericalism.

Reference has already been made to the vicar-curate relation-ship and to its intensely personal character, particularly during a young man's first curacy. The incumbent is wise to entrust a greater responsibility to the more experienced assistant curate, and it is usually a good thing when their abilities are different in range and scope; that is if their particular 'flairs' are comple-mentary and add up.

What has just been said applies equally to the relationship between the incumbent and the deaconess or woman worker, of whom there are some three hundred in parishes up and down the country. It must be admitted that many of these women experience a sense of frustration, since it is sometimes difficult for them to know precisely where they come in on the life of the parish. Often they are not given enough responsibility or treated as full members of the parochial ministry. It is up to the in-cumbent to avoid this mistake. Yet as a whole it is perhaps true to say that the Church of England is beginning to be more imaginative in its attitude to the ministry of women. Women are now at work not only in parishes, but also in universities, in moral welfare, as chaplains' assistants in hospitals and in diocesan posts: but there is still a long way to go. In the parish the right and responsible deployment of women still depends largely on the vicar.

The mature incumbent will not be jealous of gifts he does not possess, nor try to keep everything in his own hands—the sure sign of the insecure man. The temptation to regard himself as indispensable must be resisted at all costs. The sad thing is that often the less work a man does the more jealously he guards 'the rights of office'. Sometimes it is in the interests of everybody that the incumbent should have a holiday, leaving the assistant curate to carry on. It will be good for him to discover, maybe to his surprise, that the parish survives.

On the other hand, it is equally important that the assistant curate should not regard loyalty as an old-fashioned and out-moded virtue. True, if he has anything in him, he is bound to think that the vicar makes many mistakes, but there is no need for him to proclaim this from the housetop. His time will come.

The unique position of the Anglican parson, due to the historical fact that the Church of England was once the only church of the nation, means as we have seen that he accepts a responsibility for all who live within his parish. He does not only minister to a gathered congregation: he is there to serve everybody. To do this effectively, he needs to be submitted to the same conditioning factors as those around him. Parishes have their individual history, and he will wish to become sensitive to it. In this respect, residence subtly changes the nature of the personal relations into which he enters.

So it comes about that the service which the parish priest renders, what he is trying to do for the Kingdom of God, has a twofold character. These two aspects may superficially seem at variance the one with the other and suggestive of a conflict of loyalties. In fact the two duties are really one and indivisible. Indeed it is not easy to see precisely where one begins and the other ends.

First of all, the parish priest is trying to create a closely knit community around his church, the members of which consciously enter into a Christ commitment. In doing this they recognise themselves as belonging to the historic society which the life, death and resurrection of Jesus brought to birth. This society engages in corporate acts of worship, whereby it relives its inheritance and receives power for its task in the present. This community of Christ in the parish has its own life, and within itself it endeavours to lift personal relations into a higher dimension of understanding and love. Worshipping together as a family, and sharing a common life and power, its members are drawn into intimate fellowship. Such a community includes the old and the young, the good and the not so good, and its concern, both within itself and without, is to build the Kingdom of Christ. The parish priest's duty, though, of course, it is not his only, is to incarnate this Kingdom in a visible, recognisable society—the Church or *ecclesia*—known by its fruits in Christ-like living. And this particular community is the local expression of a world-wide church which has moved a long way both through space and in time.

Yet this local Christian 'cell' does not exist only for itself, for its own interior life. If it did, it would not be true to its Christ-commitment. The church is not an ark of salvation in a perishing world. Rather it is a spring-board from which to 'leap over the wall'. As Archbishop Temple has said, the church is one of the few societies which exists for non-members.

That the parochial community centred around the church needs to be closely knit and to realise its own essential unity does not imply for a moment that the distinction between *this* society and the wider society around it is clear cut and absolute. There is no iron curtain which separates the one from the other. Fortunately apartheid and segregation do not obtain here. In the same way as the parish priest has a pastoral responsibility for all who live in his parish, so the particular community over which he presides lives in and for this wider world.

Once again this view of the church is rooted in a theology which asserts that it is God's will that the whole life of man, in all its manifestations and structures, should be redeemed—that is made whole. This is what the working out of incarnation means in practice.

It is, of course, simply a matter of fact that the members of the Christian community in the parish share and are willy-nilly part of the common life of the neighbourhood around them. Their children are educated in it; they have friends there; they use its public transport, enjoy its amenities: they pay rates. In a sense they, with others, *are* it. Thus in realising their own unity, the intention is never that they should withdraw into a private club and practise a self-regarding pietism. They have a concern, as has their parish priest, with all that is happening in their own neighbourhood. They cannot be indifferent to its education, its drains, its traffic problems, its town planning, its everything. The dedicated Christian will seek to involve himself in these and similar matters, always endeavouring to introduce into their resolution the ultimate criteria of serving *persons* both in their uniqueness and in their coming together. Houses, education, safety on the roads—all these are immediately relevant since they affect the quality of the personal life in which people engage.

This does not mean that the church community any more than the parish priest has ready-made solutions to every complex problem, though amongst its members there may well be a wide knowledge. Far from it. Such solutions need to be worked out, often painfully, after long enquiry and calling upon every relevant expertise. But the Christian can hope to contribute a concern which sees every situation within the context of the personal life, and which entertains a corresponding high sense of priorities. Even here, of course, he will not claim a monopoly of vision.

I have deliberately placed an emphasis on the Christian community in the parish, although my main concern is with the parson himself. This was deliberate because the parish priest cannot be separated from the *ecclesia* within which he holds a special and significant place. In this again, he is in a different position from the doctor or lawyer who largely works through his own skill. The priest has his specialised function, and a great deal of this book is about it. Yet his task is to energise and inspire a community which, conscious of its own integrity, will engage in Christ's healing work beyond its own frontiers. This community will stretch out and seek to penetrate into the neighbourhood around, in order to serve its interests. Ceaselessly it will invade the world and resist any temptation to become preoccupied with its own life, except in so far as through such preoccupation it gains an accession of power.

It is not the parish priest's responsibility to do everything—it is an impossibility anyhow: but it is his responsibility to lead and sustain a community in such a way that it looks outwards, and becomes a real force in its own locality. By looking outwards the Christian community will in fact enrich its own interior life and in humility learn. Its members must be ready to work alongside anyone who will co-operate with them in building the Kingdom —and the Kingdom touches life at all points. The good parish priest will welcome the signs of the breaking through of a divine initiative wherever the signs of it appear, and they will appear in the secular society around him. Always, the priest is working to bring that which is outside within the Kingdom: but he will not necessarily interpret this process simply in terms

F

of church membership. His pastoral concern may properly long for such membership to increase; but to see people only as potential church-goers is not primarily to be aware of them as persons. The mature vicar will doubtless succeed (or have succeeded) in overcoming the irritation that results when people will not fit into the pattern which he thinks best for them. He will respect the other's integrity even when it sets up a resistance to his own will. Indeed he will be self-critical enough not to confuse his own desire for power with dedication to the Kingdom. Also he will be sensitive to the working of the Spirit in unexpected places. It was F. D. Maurice who said that no priest could ever dare to help others unless he believed that God's prior activity was already operative within them.

So the parish priest has a double care, but he will see these twin responsibilities as finally one. In his concern for *all* his parishioners he will not forget his responsibility to bring together a consciously committed community around the name of Jesus. In his concern for this *defined* community, he will not forget those parishioners who are in a sense outside it but who are not entirely untouched by the activity of the in-dwelling Christ.

It is now time to look a little more closely at the particular tasks which the parson undertakes as he discharges his double responsibility, which is really one.

CHAPTER 5

IN SICKNESS AND IN HEALTH

THERE are certain areas of his work where the double responsibility of the parish priest seems obviously to overlap, and it will therefore be as well to deal with these 'bridges' first. Such areas, and this will not seem surprising in view of what has been suggested earlier, arise from the inheritance into which he has entered. Despite the contemporary break-away from faith, it is still true that the parish priest comes into intimate association with a large number of his parishioners, and this at the most significant moments in their lives—at birth, marriage and death. For a vast majority of people, indeed for nearly everybody, these represent occasions when something of significance seems to happen in them quite independently of whether they make any religious profession. There has, it is true, been a decrease of late years, but still 55 per cent of the babies born in England in 1960 were baptised according to the rites of the Church of England, and 47 per cent of the marriages in England in 1962 were solemnised according to these rites.

The birth of a baby usually evokes feelings of awe, of wonder, and of joy. In its absolute dependence upon its mother, the baby 'does something' not only to the parents but to the wider family into which it is introduced. Such an elemental experience of itself generates the urge to thanksgiving and prompts a quickened sense of dedication and responsibility. And this happens not because anyone says it ought to, but in the nature of the case. The event elicits this kind of response in normal human nature.

It is in part because of this that the Christian church, enriching a tradition which is older than Christianity itself, invites parents and the community to give thanks, to respond to a call to duty, and to introduce the young baby into the life of the Christian family. The service of baptism (together with that of thanksgiving after childbirth) speak to the mood of a real human situation and address themselves to a felt need. To engage in acts of this kind is what many people feel they want to do at such a time.

No one would or could pretend that all the babies that are baptised come from homes where the parents entertain a clear and settled Christian intention. It is well to be reminded that many such baptisms represent the survival of an almost primitive superstition, or the opportunity for a social occasion. Indeed there may even be a hangover, so persistent are collective patterns of behaviour, from days when baptism was a legal requirement and the only way of registering a birth. Such may well be the case, and it is for this reason that parish priests rightly try to see that the parents understand what baptism, in a Christian context, is about, and that the god-parents, or at least one of them, is an active communicant member of the Church of England. Yet it would be as unwise as it would be superficial to write off what has been described as indiscriminate baptism in terms of a mere façade, a shadow lacking substance. Human motives are very complex and self-knowledge in respect of them is rare. Many parents, without being fully aware of what has happened or been effected in them, do experience through the birth of their baby some call to an idealism not heard before, the stirring of a quickened sensitivity leading to a desire to do the best for this helpless infant mysteriously entrusted to them. They glimpse an end beyond 'getting and spending'. In this chastened mood, they tend to assume, though the assumption is often inarticulate, that the Christian church stands for just this kind of assertion. They would wish, may be vaguely, to associate themselves with it, and perhaps not quite so vaguely, their children. To them baptism does not appear artificial because its implications have not been thought through, nor as hollow as a critique of their precise conscious motivation might seem to suggest. Indeed it seems an expression of what they have come to know.

To this parental mood, baptism in its most simple form addresses itself, and it is perhaps a great pity in this respect that the service in the Book of Common Prayer is so unnecessarily obscure as well as being theologically 'off putting'. The symbolism of water and the sign of the cross, however, still conveys meaning, as does the receiving of a name.

One thing is quite certain. It is that for the parish priest, active as he must be in building the Kingdom, baptism provides a unique pastoral opportunity so far as the parents, the godparents, their family and friends, and on occasions his own congregation, are concerned—assuming that he is a big enough man to be able to come in on it. To have baptised a baby, even when the parents are not, as is said, committed Christians undoubtedly creates a potential and real link between him and the family, and, of course, with the baby as he grows up. This link is none the less real because it is difficult to define or to put into words. Every parish priest knows this from his own experience. Moreover, baptism gives to him and to the community of which he is a focal point, a responsibility and he will make the most of this. Usually—it is here that the excessively large parish can be a frustration—he will visit the parents before the baptism so that they can be helped to understand its significance, and also that he may get to know them and they him. He will discuss the matter of god-parents, so that they are not regarded merely as a routine requirement. On rare occasions he will offer to provide one from his own congregation. He will hope, together with the community centred around him, to keep in touch with the family and to engraft the baby effectively into the life of the Christian fellowship. Where the parish priest maintains such an interest, the parents seldom regard it as an intrusion. They welcome his involvement in the family situation.

The vicar of a parish is required to baptise those who are brought to him, and at his institution he promises to seek out the unbaptised and to engraft them into the Christian community. There are those—and very dedicated people they are—who pour scorn on what they describe as 'indiscriminate baptism in a post-Christian age', by which is meant baptism from a non-Christian home where neither parents nor god-parents seem to have any definite Christian intention. Of course it must be the parish priest's responsibility, in so far as he can, to see that such an intention exists and, where it does not, to foster it. Yet he may be wise to recognise that in life as it is, and not as he would ideally wish it to be, baptism (as in the early days of the Anglo-Saxon church) may precede and indeed lead to the 'conversion' of the parents: and that the link which he has forged through the intimacies of the ceremony itself may have the effect of creating the most enduring relationship with the family.

Once again, life is more subtle than a formal logic might suggest and the most lax parent or god-parent, through the grace of God, may come to a Christian conviction under the suasion of his new responsibilities. Who knows? Certainly a strong formal case can be made for the fencing in of baptism and for making it as discriminate as a consistent theological logic can contrive: but the refusal or even the conditional refusal to baptise, though the theoretical position may be unassailable, will usually irritate and be misunderstood. It will not be seen, though in reality it usually is, as arising from a deep desire to secure the greatest possible benefit for the child, while at the same time maintaining the integrity of both church and parents: but as an effort to remove the church just one stage further away and withdraw its benefits from ordinary people. The parents will probably be hurt just at a time when they might become suggestible. Aristotle had something relevant to say when he urged that we must take people as they are if we wish to make them what they ought to be—though this cautionary note smacks a little of a very superior presumption. The world is bedevilled by people who want to make others what they ought to be! There is, however, a great deal to be said, I am sure, particularly in an Established Church which has (until fairly recent times) little tradition of a gathered congregation, for the parish priest seeing his duty in the widest possible context, though to act in response to such liberality may often leave him a little ill at ease. Still it is not his peace of mind which matters most, but service to the Kingdom. Let it be said, of course, that baptism which is indiscriminate through sheer laziness, or the unwillingness ever to make a stand, is another matter. I am not talking about this.

It is ordered in the Book of Common Prayer that the parish priest shall hold baptism after the second lesson in Morning

Prayer. The reason for this requirement is simple. The baby is being introduced into the Christian family, and the compilers of the Prayer Book wished to secure that this family was present when the baptism took place, and the largest congregation was present in the morning. To-day public baptism has been slowly converted into semi-private baptism and though a practical and psychological case can be made for this change, it is not wholly a good thing. Efforts are now being made to ensure that once again baptisms should be held 'in the face of the congregation'. A too doctrinaire approach here, however, has its complications. In cases of serious illness, the priest often baptises the baby at the parents' home or in hospital, in which case the infant is later received into the Christian community at a short service in church.

Baptisms are entered into a register, and a card usually given to the parents. Many churches now have baptismal rolls which lead to regular visits from members of the congregation. Perhaps it may be added that there is legal provision for the changing of Christian names at baptism.

Baptism in the Church of England is not confined to the young. Often the parish priest prepares adults, but here it is usually the immediate prelude to confirmation, which is an entering into full adult responsibility in the life of the church.

The service of 'Churching' is not so popular as it once was, partly because it used to be geared to a somewhat primitive idea of ritual cleansing, which so long as it was believed in proved a powerful incentive. To-day the emphasis is on thanksgiving after childbirth, and the parish priest tries to secure that the father (usually shy and reluctant) as well as the mother is present.

If birth is for most people a 'numinous' experience, so is marriage. No human relationship more powerfully expresses the essential nature of a truly personal order than the life-long and loyal commitment which marriage represents and embodies. Perhaps this is because the aura in which lovers behold each other reflects the aura in which the 'Divine Lover' beholds the uniqueness of every man. Only the dullness of our blinded sight prevents us from seeing all people as bathed in this light.

'God gives all men all earth to love, But since man's heart is small,
Ordains for each, one spot should prove, Beloved over all.'

Once again, the parish priest has the privilege of 'coming in' on this elemental experience. Falling in love can constitute a great awakening; an opening of the eyes; a new realisation of what commitment is, and personal loyalty can become. And this again is 'given'. It is not injected by homilies on the nature of marriage, but arises from within the experience of personal encounter out of which marriage springs. The promises taken when the lovers plight their troth to each other are not imposed upon them reluctantly against their will. Indeed vows less demanding, less absolute, would at the time fall lamentably below the level of their own intense feelings for each other. Nothing less exalted is adequate to the expression of their mutual love.

'And I will luve thee still, my dear, Till a' the seas gang dry.'

Marriage, therefore, offers a unique pastoral opportunity of incalculable worth to the sensitive parish priest. Indeed, he may himself catch a contagion, and renew a hope, from these ardent lovers' dedication to each other. Thomas Hardy wrote some of his best love poetry when he was over seventy!

As in baptism, the motives of the 47 per cent of people who specifically desire to come to the Church of England for their marriage are probably very mixed but they must be seen against the background of what I have suggested above. It is, I believe, only too understandable that many young people should wish to be married in church quite independently of whether they make any conscious or formal profession of Christian Faith. The nature of the experience into which they have entered naturally leads to an expression of it in some symbolic and ritual act. There is a felt need 'to tell it out abroad' that they love each other, since their encounter looks without as well as within. It seems right that their own, and society's recognition of their personal relationship—since it has enormous social implications, indeed will probably lead to the creation of a new society— should be represented through acts and thought forms which clearly give it a wider reference. Of course this does not gainsay the fact that many who wish to be married in church do so simply because it gives a kind of glamour—but then marriage is glamorous: others because it seems more respectable, more colourful, particularly when the church is set in a rather delightful rural scene, a 'proper wedding' with an aisle to walk up in white. Yet even such motives are not to be entirely despised or written off, for they represent an awareness that this is no ordinary occasion, but has a life significance. The wedding at a registrar's office—in spite of the noble endeavours of many a registrar—is inadequate to meet the deep emotional involvement of those concerned, though it is legally all that is required. It seems a wedding minus, and the minus is not the less a real lack because it represents an imponderable.

Parishioners, that is those who are resident in a parish, or are on the church electoral roll,* have a right to be married in their parish church and the parish priest has a corresponding duty to make the church available and either to marry them himself or to see that someone else does so. The priest conducts the marriage on the authority of either banns which have been published in church on three successive Sundays (this is the most usual way); by a special licence granted by the Archbishop of Canterbury; an ordinary licence from the bishop;† or a certificate issued by a superintendent registrar.

Purely legal requirements of this kind make it necessary for the parish priest to 'come in' on the lives of his parishioners in a way which is in no sense artificial. In this respect the incumbent acts as a civil officer—a registrar. He himself either personally or through his clerk takes particulars of banns, publishes them, and issues a certificate that this has been done. He keeps a register of marriages (two in fact) which he signs, gives a certificate to the newly married, and sends regular returns to Somerset House. Here is an excellent example of the *mixta persona* of the parish priest, as also, for example, when he

---

* See p. 107.

† Some clergymen in each diocese are appointed as surrogates, and this authorises them to take down the particulars of a marriage, swear the affidavit, so that the diocesan registrar may issue the licence.

witnesses signatures on innumerable governmental forms. I believe that there is great value in the civil official being also a religious person. Here he represents what is essentially true of every man, and this double function reminds us how false is the distinction that we so often make between the sacred and the secular.

Nearly every parish priest now sees the couple before their marriage at least once. This gives him the opportunity of making himself personally known to them; to take them through the service; to suggest some thoughts as to the Christian attitude to marriage (this can be overdone, because often the couple have already arrived there!); and to be generally helpful. He may suggest that they read some such publication as that excellent little pamphlet *The Threshold of Marriage*. The wise parson understands that though he has taken many marriages before, he has never before taken *this* one. It (with every marriage) is a unique event. There is all the difference in the world between a marriage geared to a pastoral concern, which seems to arise within the life history of the two people immediately involved, and that which suggests a routine operation with the young couple merely representative objects entering into the estate of matrimony. The preparation for the ceremony and the ceremony itself ought to reflect the hopes and ideals of two unique persons. It is the responsibility of the parish priest to measure up to the aspirations of those getting married, and in the rare cases where such aspiration is low he must try to make it higher. One thing is certain, moralising in itself will not get very far, nor the hearty sentimentality sometimes resorted to. Fortunately the marriage service itself provides a structure around which a serious discussion can take place; while such questions as the choice of appropriate music help to introduce a necessary practicality. Perhaps it should be said that, if he is wise, the parish priest will never miss an opportunity of going to the reception after the marriage—if he is invited. His presence enables him to enter into the mood of the total event and this will be appreciated and remembered afterwards. Perhaps it is equally important that he should know when to depart!

Marriage illustrates again how a necessary duty imposed upon the parish priest by virtue of his office can become the means of creating a unique relationship between him and his parishioners, thereby helping him in his task of building a truly personal order. It is in the family that early loyalties cluster and right relationships grow. The church itself *is* a family, the household of God.

Perhaps a word may be—indeed must be—included about the priest and the marriage of divorced persons while a former partner is still living. Though according to the law of the land he is perfectly in order in marrying such people—and a very few clergymen do—no priest himself can be required to conduct such a marriage, nor to allow his church to be used for this purpose. Resolutions of convocation and episcopal directions go further and forbid clergy to conduct any such marriages in church. The whole matter is a subject of controversy, and many clergy (like myself) are critical of the 'official Church view'. But two things may be said irrespective of such differences. All Anglican clergy accept that they have a responsibility for their parishioners, including those who have remarried or wish to remarry after divorce. Such a behaviour pattern does not take away from the parish priest's pastoral concern. Most bishops encourage their clergy, in accordance with resolutions of convocation, to pray with a couple who, after divorce, have remarried in a registrar's office—that is, when such prayer is asked for and seems appropriate. It is only right to say that those who hold a rigorist attitude, as it is sometimes called, are motivated by a deep concern for the welfare of people, and by loyalty to the teaching of Christ and the traditions of the Church as they understand them.

It would be improper, however, in this book, to go into the theological arguments which lie behind this discussion. Where, I repeat, there is absolute agreement amongst all parish priests is that they have a pastoral care for the divorced, just as much as for those whose married life has either proved more equable or, if it has not, divorce has not been resorted to as a remedy. The mature parish priest is never shocked; nor has he an obsessive neurosis about sexual irregularity as if it constituted the worst or the only sin. He knows from experience, and it expresses itself in his ministry, that 'there but for the grace of God goes John Wesley'. He is aware that even in the seemingly worst of human situations there is often some dim striving after the good, some endeavour, be it never so misguided, to discover the sacred. This does not mean, as superficially it might be thought to mean, that the priest plays fast and loose with his own and with what he regards as Christian standards: only that his standards relate to the fulfilment of persons in their relations with each other—persons whom he believes have the great dignity of being created in the image of God. Perhaps it should be added that in the Church of England divorced people are not automatically excommunicated and thus for ever denied the sacraments.

The third occasion on which the parish priest is involved in the intimate family life of his parishioners is at death.

There was a time when every parishioner had a right (except in very exceptional circumstances) to be buried in the church-yard. That day of necessity has passed. Most churchyards are now full, and burials, except in some small country parishes, usually take place in cemeteries. Crematoria are more and more being used, and often the ashes are scattered. The monopoly of the Church of England parson has rightly disappeared, and to-day Free Church ministers and Roman Catholic priests officiate at the burial of members of their own flock.

The position now is—and this is a legacy of the traditions of an older age—that any parishioner who asks his vicar to officiate at a burial will always receive the answer that he will be privi-leged to do so. When the deceased is a member of his own congregation, or is known to him, he will probably suggest that the body be brought into the church for the first part of the burial service. But no parishioner, whether he is a church-goer or not, would ever be refused this ministry. Of course to-day, in areas where the population is dense, it is difficult for the vicar always to know that a death has taken place. When he does know he will visit the family: and when he cannot be expected to know, it is to be hoped he will be told. It is for this, and for many other reasons, that some parishes have instituted a system of 'street leaders' (familiar as part of civil defence during the last war).

It is of course a great privilege to share the life of a family at the time of bereavement: but how helpful this sharing will prove must largely depend on whether the parish priest has the insight and force of character to make it so. Certainly he has an initial advantage in what he stands for and represents. When death strikes a family, it often brings with it a sense of acute and at times paralysing personal loss, sometimes a feeling of protest. It can momentarily slow down the pace of life, and raises ultimate questions which have not been faced up to for years. A true pastor, who is the trustee of a 'sure and certain hope', ought to be able to bring a measure of healing to those caught up in such grief.

But there is no need to repeat in this context what I have already said in respect of baptism and marriage. Families do appreciate interest and concern at a time of bereavement, and most people do not feel that the parish priest is intruding on a private grief when he tries to identify himself with them in this situation. Certainly an anonymous funeral, by which I mean when both the deceased and the bereaved are unknown to the 'officiating minister', usually seems to lack an essential element, though there are occasions when this anonymity is unavoidable.

A parish priest is expected to visit and minister to the sick: or to put this the other way round, the sick of the parish have a right to his ministrations. In the Book of Common Prayer there is a special service for this purpose, and when England was, in the main, a collection of small villages this order was regularly used.

The particular reason for imposing this duty upon the parish priest arose within an older historical and theological context. In early centuries, sickness was usually regarded as a punishment for sin, certainly as a divine chastening: and at a time when scientific medical diagnosis did not exist, any illness was seen as possibly fatal. It was important to secure a death-bed repentance since this could effect a man's destiny throughout eternity. Hence the intercession in the Litany to be delivered from 'sudden' death. To-day we are right to reject such theological propositions; yet this does not alter the fact that sickness can often be a time for spiritual recreation, when the busy routine of life is broken into, and in the pause that follows things happen in a man. He has leisure; he is dependent upon others; he experiences a new sense of need. A pastor can be helpful, not by trying to induce a heightened religious response, but by endeavouring to interpret the person to himself, through sensitivity to his present mood and condition.

With increasing awareness in our days of how the mind (I use this for want of a better term) reacts on the body and *vice versa*, the priest may well have his part to play alongside the doctor in the whole process of healing. The use of such a phrase as 'psychosomatic' is a reminder that to try to heal the body whilst still leaving the person restless and disturbed in himself is to risk and invite a recurrence of the original malady. It is to life and wholeness that every man is called, and the parish priest is the representative of that Christ who said: 'I have come that men may have life, and may have it in all its fullness.' Though an older theology is now rightly discredited, the parish priest does not become irrelevant at the bedside of the sick or when ministering to the dying. It is, of course, not his task to usurp the functions of the doctor nor to embark on the deep analysis of the psychiatrist, except in so far as he is qualified to do so. He is there as a pastor and priest to deal with the whole person. It is an encouraging sign of the times that clergy and doctors are in many areas getting together. Indeed some fifty-five groups have been set up in various parts of the country.*

Visiting is one of the most important duties which the parish priest undertakes, and should be high on his list of priorities. There is no alternative to it. It used to be said that a parson was as much out of place in his parish in the morning as he would be in his study in the afternoon. Times have changed somewhat since these words were written but the principle is a sound one. Now that women are often out at work during the day and 'tele' is obsessional in the evening, it is not always easy to find the

* See *Clergy-Doctor Co-operation*, A Report. Church Information, April 1963.

right time. But where there's a will there's a way: and in order to get to know a person intimately there is nothing like visiting him in his own home. There he expands, is often ready to talk, and is more likely to be himself. The old, if they are to be known at all, must often be sought out, and it is important to do this, for, in the hurry and bustle of modern life, they can easily be by-passed. They should be of special concern to the parson of the parish and he will find time spent with them amply repaid. Old people, if only we will allow them to talk and reminisce, are usually most interesting to those who have ears to hear.

This kind of personal ministry may not seem exciting (though people *are* exciting) and have little news value. But it is a desperately important occupation for the parish priest.

Here, I repeat, is a unique ministry. It may not still be true that a house-going parson makes a church-going people: but it is true that time spent in this way is never wasted, and that the parish priest ought to see himself in this matter as a 'representative person'. One is reminded of Geoffrey Chaucer's 'poor parson of a town'. Though in densely populated areas the incumbent and his assistant curates cannot hope to visit other than a relatively small percentage of their people, this is no reason for declining to undertake the task at all. All or nothing is too easy a solution of a very real problem. The good visitor is sensitive to particular situations, for example when to stay and when to depart. Normally (I believe), except when sickness is the reason for the call, a first visit needs to be long enough to make possible a really effective personal encounter. People are not like Melchizedek, who was without ancestry; they are usually better known by the priest when he is aware of their background and personal history. The good visitor is a good listener, and does his best to identify himself with, or at least to understand the mood of, the parishioner he has called on. It is obvious, for example, that a widow whose only son lives, shall we say, in America, cannot really be known, apart from an awareness of this personal situation. Also, if a facetious exaggeration may be pardoned, to many an old person, concern for an arthritic knee takes initial priority over the successful working of U.N.O. Here is the 'way in'. It is right that the parish priest should offer friendship, and on occasions quiet a troubled conscience whether through a formal confession with absolution, or by informal discussion—or both.

Such visiting, of course, need not and should not be confined to church-goers and their special needs—as for example to take the sacrament of Holy Communion to their own homes. The opportunities for more general visits are endless, since in every parish people have their own life history, with their stresses and strains, their sorrows and rejoicings. Though, as I shall suggest later, the incumbent must penetrate into the 'structures' of his neighbourhood, nothing can replace the day-to-day visiting of individual persons and families in their own homes.

Nor will the parish priest be the only person to undertake this responsibility. He will encourage members of his congregation to share it with him, but in doing this he must undoubtedly recognise that his own visits will be felt to have a special significance because of his more representative capacity.

A few words must be added in this context concerning the Parish Magazine or News Letter. Here is a unique opportunity, through the printed word, for the Church and its message to penetrate into homes which, maybe, the Vicar himself does not enter. Since this is so, it is essential that this publication should really say something; that it should have a cutting edge and be relevant, not giving an over-all impression of triviality. Certainly its general appearance should be professional. The incumbent will be wise to seek the best advice and associate others with him in this enterprise. If he can make his Magazine of service to the interests of the wider community so much the better. The sad fact is that so often the opportunity to do this is frittered away.

CHAPTER 6

THE CHRISTIAN FAMILY

MY concern, in the last chapter, was with the duties of the
parish priest at those points where they cut right across the
distinction between what he does when ministering to his
own congregation and when ministering to all and sundry
within the boundaries of his parish. It is not only the baby
born into a church-going family that he baptises; nor only
church-goers that he marries, or finally lays to rest. He visits
widely.

It is important, however, that we should now turn to his
particular task in ministering to that worshipful community
which (so we believe) God is calling together and seeking to
strengthen through him. This community can never, if true
to itself, become inward looking or self-preserving. It is always
overflowing and endeavouring to penetrate into the territories
and structures of the common life. At the same time, and in
order to do this effectively, it needs to be given cohesion; it must
realise its own integrity; it must see itself as a 'cell' in a living
Christian organism which stretches out through time and
space. This community bears distinctive witness to a particular
commitment which is expressed (or ought to be) in the shape
and pattern of its own inner life. Within this community the
parish priest holds a unique place, and though he believes in,
and works to give expression to, the priesthood of all believers,
he cannot alter the historico-empirical fact (based, many would
affirm, on a theological truth) that he has a particular and
representative function to discharge which unless he discharges
it goes by default. In this respect the Church of England is not a
democratic institution as that word is popularly understood.
The parish priest has always been central in the life of the local
Christian community, and not only in respect of his ministering
the word and sacrament which he is commissioned to do by

the bishop. If he is not adequate to his unique responsibilities, then the whole community suffers and is impoverished. If he is lethargic, stale and frustrated, in some odd way this seems to impregnate the community and infect even its worship. Perhaps the day will come when a live parish will carry, indeed be able to revitalise and recreate, from within its own faith and loyalty, its ineffective parson, but this day is not yet. Even if it were to come, it would still be true that the parish priest, because of his status as a *mixta persona*, is in a unique position to give leadership.

One of the functions which belongs *sui generis* to him as a priest is the leading of his people in public worship in the parish church, where he ministers both the word and the sacraments. It is not intended, however, that this book should discuss at any length the theology of such corporate activity nor the structure of the services in the Book of Common Prayer. What must be said here, however, is that the reverent and alive offering of a relevant worship must always be one of the over-riding preoccupations of the parish priest. Worship, in this sense, offered in the name and according to the intention of Jesus, is no extra to the community's life, no odd eccentricity for queer people, though doubtless there is need to move towards a contemporary form for its more adequate expression, using the best of the modern images which poet and artist can bring to this generation.

Essentially worship arises from man's awareness of his dependence upon God, and from the sense of awe and wonder which this creaturely experience brings with it. Yet Christian worship is more than a response to God's 'Otherness', a recognition that he is the Supreme Mystery whose 'thoughts are not our thoughts neither his ways our ways'. Christian worship embodies a conviction that God is active in Jesus, and that this activity is directed towards our fulfilment as persons. Hence Christians are encouraged to address God as Father, and their worship is the offering of a family, the members of which celebrate with thankfulness the historic life of their own community, stretching back as it does in time to the days when the Word became flesh. Events in the past become meaningful in the present as believers identify themselves with their Lord in His life, death and mighty resurrection.

It is certainly no part of this 'group exercise' that it should be antiquarian in character, the nostalgic remembrance of a long lost hero. Rather the worshipper, aware of the intrinsic 'worship' of God, who is the source and sustainer of all value, knows himself in this experience to be confronting a reality which he cannot use or manipulate to his own ends, as we do all too often in our human encounters. For this reason worship is therapeutic; it reminds us of our real human situation; it gives vision, cleanses, and releases power.

The parish priest, under the bishop as 'ordinary', is responsible for the worship of his church, and he conducts this, in the main, in accordance with the Book of Common Prayer, though the particular manner of his doing this will vary from church to church. The 1662 Prayer Book, in spite of its great beauty of language and depth of insight, stands desperately in need of revision,* or, perhaps better, of being used alongside other and more modern orders of worship. Yet even as it is, it can become far more meaningful, and a world of difference is made, when the parish priest shows care, interest and imagination. The quality of music, the elocution, the choice of hymns, the character of the additional prayers, the dignity of movement, the aesthetics of the vestments—all these are important and add to the reality of the total worshipful experience, not only when the Book of Common Prayer is used but also in such special services as are held on Mothering Sunday, Harvest Festival, Remembrance Day—occasions when 'non-church-goers' are usually present.

This ordering of public worship is a great responsibility. Theological statements (that is truths about God and man) are more likely to become meaningful when they are expressed in symbolic and ritual forms than when they are made a subject of formal discussion. The service of Holy Communion, the Lord's Supper, the Mass or Eucharist—call it what you will—illustrates this truth, for it is the unfolding of a real drama expressive of the life, death and resurrection of Jesus. Something

* Such a revision was attempted in 1928.

is 'done' in the present which has its counterpart in eternity, and it is not surprising, therefore, that this worshipful act has attracted to itself a veritable wealth of artistic creation.

In ordering worship, the parish priest will seek help and guidance from many sources—from his organist, for example— and he will discuss the matter with his parishioners and take them into his confidence. But this is an area in which he ought to have a measure of expert knowledge, applied (we may hope!) with a degree of commonsense. Finally he must use his own judgment, particularly when it is a matter of being sensitive to the needs of his own parishioners. Patterns of worship vary from parish to parish according to different traditional (and sometimes individual) ways of interpreting the services in the Book of Common Prayer. The pastoral parish priest does not begin by flouting his congregation in matters of this kind, though this does not mean that there is no need for change, indeed for bold experimentation outside the Book of Common Prayer altogether. Indeed I think there is. But it does mean that there is a pastoral way of embarking upon this, so as to respect the other person, and be sensitive even to his prejudice, though this must not hold up the course of change. A dignified spoken service, with everyone playing his part, will be appropriate for some very small congregations: it will certainly be inappropriate for most others. What is essential is that everything should induce a mood out of which a true worship easily springs: that the whole offering should be as worthy in its intention, both theological and aesthetic, as can be contrived. It may be natural to worship, but it is not necessarily natural to worship well.

It is the parish priest's responsibility by his own deportment, sustained interest, and meticulous care to encourage his congregation to see that the worship he leads really matters; and that as a consequence nothing in it is slovenly, perfunctory or slipshod.

Organically related to a worship, which is at its heart sacramental, is the proclamation of the word. The preaching ministry is not an optional extra but has its part to play within the whole life of the church. It is in itself an 'event'. True the sermon has become the butt of every man's wit in its soporific content, its platitudinous character, its ineffectiveness. Such criticisms are valuable (and alas! often only too well merited), particularly when they prompt to greater effort and more careful preparation. The fact is, of course, that to have to preach every Sunday (sometimes two different sermons) is an arduous responsibility and many people are just not up to it. Yet it is an opportunity which comes the way of no other profession, and its survival into the twentieth century is almost miraculous. Once again it is in part an historical legacy from a semi-illiterate age. This does not mean, however, that preaching should be written off but rather adapted to a contemporary situation and used to the best advantage. 'In the beginning was the preacher'; and one only has to know something of the preaching of the early friars or in later times of Whitfield or John Wesley to realise its potential power.

The function of the sermon is to proclaim the good news of the Christian Gospel, what it is, and what God does through it. This demands that the preacher handles and explicates present and immediate human experience. There must be no suggestion in the sermon that the Christian Faith is an historic relic, which has somehow gone on because there are too many vested interests to allow anyone to stop it. What God did He does still, and the preacher must assume that He is active in every man, even though every man may build up resistances to His effective working.

Certainly the preacher in the parish church begins with some initial advantages. He knows or ought to know his own people, and they him. He has (we hope) been into their homes. He is caught up in the particularities of the same local, national and international scene. Here, in this living day-to-day experience in which God is already working, the Christian Gospel becomes relevant and alive. It must, of course, have first come alive in the preacher himself.

The parish priest has a duty to proclaim the Faith, and to do this within patterns of worship. This does not necessarily demand gifts of eloquence—though these can be an asset—but it certainly means care, thought and time given to it; the perennial stretching of the preacher's own mind so that he does not grow stale and atrophied; a sensitivity to people. He must know what is going on in the world around him and equally within himself. To read widely is an essential tool of his trade.

The sermon is no longer almost the only universal educative medium, and in this sense it has lost something of its older significance: but this does not mean that it has lost its relevance. The tragedy is that the opportunity is so often frittered away, not so much through sheer incompetence as from a failure imaginatively to realise how important the exercise can be. It is not the preacher's task either to give odd comments on the week's news, though the week's news can be desperately important in a sermon, or to provide his congregation with the doubtful benefits of whatever happens to come into his mind the moment he stands up. Preaching is a serious business and those who are listening expect, need, and deserve to be given something serious and *sui generis* to the occasion. What is right elsewhere may not necessarily be what is required here. Certainly at a time when people are exposed to all kinds of persuasives on the radio and in print it is essential that the sermon should be geared to its primary objective. The preacher must be recognised as under a constraint; he is a commissioned man, and as such he must expect to be used, and used most effectively when he has done his best to prepare himself for his task. In a sense every sermon is a unique event, both in itself and in relation to those to whom it is directed. It should form a part of the total worshipful act. At all costs the preacher must respect the intelligence and integrity of the members of his congregation. He is there to build up and not to break down. He needs to give a reason for the hope that is within him, believing that the whole man must be dedicated to God and that this cannot happen if the mind is not ministered to as well as the heart.

There is still a place, I repeat, for the sermon if it keeps within its own terms of reference: but there is no place for the ill-prepared, badly constructed discourse unrelated to a dynamically challenging Christian Faith. There is no value in the sermon which is phonetic only, for example, when the preacher imagines something to be said merely because he is using particular words that were once charged with a highly emotional content. Some have experimented with a dialogue in place of the sermon, leading into later discussion. The restored church of St. Mary-le-Bow has two pulpits!

It is unnecessary here to go into detail as to the nature and scope of the worshipful life of the community for which the parish priest is responsible. Such a life will express itself in many forms, in small groups as well as in large; and it will arise out of the community's rich and manifold corporate existence. The exciting parish priest will instruct himself, and others, in techniques of prayer in respect of which a vast deal of expertise from the East is now available in the West. It is encouraging that so many 'cells' for this purpose are springing up spontaneously in so many parishes.

As part of this worshipful offering—and it *is* a part of it—there is the building in which, in the main, it takes place, the church. Of course, genuine Christian worship can take place wherever two or three are gathered together in the name of Jesus: but the importance of the physical habitat within which the community brings to a focal point its corporate and worshipful life can hardly be exaggerated. Here is the visible, sacramental expression of the community's existence, a continuing symbol. Often the building is itself the embodiment of a local history in which all can take a pride. Medieval churches have been described as acts of worship in stone, and this applies (at least in intention) to churches of other periods and types of architecture. The actual structure and form of the building, together with its furnishings, ought themselves to be expressive of man's aspiration after God and the 'givenness' of God's response to that aspiration.

In respect both of church and the churchyard around it the incumbent has a special charge. The freehold is vested in him, though it is held in joint possession of the incumbent and the parochial church council. (The churchwardens are owners of the moveables.) This means that the responsibility for the upkeep of the church is a shared one and the wise parish priest will be quick to recognise and take advantage of this fact. The parish churches of our land are a unique inheritance both historical as well as architectural, and it is to be hoped that those in process of being built will prove to be so for future generations. Their interest is far wider than the Christian community. Indeed many people contribute to their upkeep who make no religious profession. By their beauty and the associations which cluster around them they speak to all and sundry.

Yet though the maintenance of the church is a shared responsibility, almost everything in practice, and this is inevitable, will depend upon the parish priest, on whether he regards his stewardship as an embarrassing chore or on the other hand sustains his own interest, seeks the best advice, and is alive to the real purpose of the building. To energise others to take a pride in it he must first show a pride in it himself, and this means lavishing both care and imagination upon it. In this respect the parish priest has a full-time preoccupation. He is always, as we say, on the spot and can give to the building a concentrated attention. A badly kept church, untidy, with chairs stacked away in odd corners, tawdry furnishings, old flower vases (usually green), ragged hymn-books, inadequate lighting, dirty linen, out of date notices—can anything be more desolating than these? Equally unfortunate is the building which betrays only too clearly that no interest has been taken in its history and little in its present deployment. Fortunately most churches are not like this, but where they are, the incumbent must be held responsible. That they are not is an indication that parish priests are taking their charge more seriously and that Diocesan Advisory Boards are beginning to be effective. Also dioceses insist on periodic architectural inspection.

It must be admitted that the upkeep of an ancient building, often large, may well exceed the resources of a small village and can be a real headache to a parish priest, particularly where there has been neglect over a long period of years. In spite of visitations by both rural deans and archdeacons, all too often the attitude in the past seems to have been, 'Never do to-day what can possibly be put off till to-morrow'. Indeed the upkeep can constitute such a preoccupation around the raising of money—and this in spite of help from the Historic Churches

Preservation Trust and diocesan grants—that the worried incumbent begins to wonder what he is in the parish for. Yet this *cri de coeur* can be somewhat exaggerated.* True, the vicar's task is not primarily to act as the custodian of an ancient building, but this is to misconceive the nature and purpose of the building itself and the trust reposed in him. If the church really is the home of a worshipful and vital community, of great contemporary significance as well as having a venerable past behind it, then the psychological reaction to the upkeep of the building becomes quite different. The imaginative incumbent will be quick to realise that the building itself has something to say to passers-by: and that it can become a home for all that 'is lovely and of good report'—for music and the arts.

With the upkeep of the church is associated the care of the parish registers, and records generally. The former may go back to Elizabethan times, when such registers were first required, and they constitute a unique repository of local history. The incumbent should see that they are kept safe and dry, and he might encourage a scholar to calendar them and put them in order. Often they shed light on national affairs in their casual references to people who were, or later became, famous. The history of England is in part the story of what happened to ordinary people in the parishes. Facilities are now available in many dioceses for the micro-filming of these irreplaceable records and the conscientious incumbent will see that this is done, if possible.

What has been said of such records applies equally to other treasures which the church may possess—for example flagons, chalices, memorials† and hatchments. Not only ought these to be carefully guarded but from time to time exhibited. If the

---

* I myself believe that it would be possible, if the right initiative were taken, for state aid to become available for all such ancient buildings, as happens on the continent. This need not lead to governmental control any more than it does in the case of the B.B.C. or the universities.

† I must confess that I do not share the modern prejudice against memorials in church. Often they add to interest, and are an embodiment of parish history.

vicar can persuade some competent person to write a history of the church and parish—perhaps he might attempt it himself —he will have done well.

Once again, this particular responsibility enables the parish priest to root himself in the community, and to enter into personal relations beyond his immediate congregation.

What has been said of the church applies equally to the churchyard around it. Nothing looks worse than an ill-kept churchyard, yet how difficult it is to keep up! Difficult but not impossible when an energetic and concerned vicar determines to do something about it.

The incumbent in these and other matters is in a position of leadership and until the pattern of Anglicanism drastically changes he is likely to remain so. He cannot easily be by-passed. If he has the capacity for inspiring others, he will discover that they can be provoked into being as responsible as himself. The fact that both socially and theologically the parish has across the years been geared to its parson means an almost excessive reliance on him, so much so that if he is inactive little seems to happen and there is frustration all round. There are, however, various kinds of leadership; and there is all the difference in the world between the leader who smothers everyone else, sapping their vitality while wishing them to fall in behind him, and the kind of leadership which evokes a virile response and encourages initiative in others. The first is deplorable. A real leader excites a lively comeback because he is prepared to welcome this reaction as a condition of creative growth and the means by which highly particularised persons make their best contributions. It is to the right kind of leadership that the parish priest is called, and its exercise becomes significant when he seeks to bring his worshipful community into a consciousness of itself as a family—a truly personal order. That there is a need to do this is a practical recognition that church and parish or more properly church and neighbourhood are not synonymous, and that a Christian commitment demands a positive dedication. To make a selfconscious community of committed Christians is not in any sense to encourage introversion or to pluck brands from the burning. This self-awareness is necessary just in order that the Christian community can look outwards from a real centre.

It is perhaps worth noticing that since the Parochial Church Councils Measure, 1921,* this differentiated Christian community has been given legal recognition, and it was for this reason that Bishop Hensley Henson objected to the Measure. Under this legislation an electoral roll was established upon which laymen are eligible over the age of seventeen, if they are baptised members of the Church of England and resident in the parish; or, if non-resident, have habitually attended the church for six months. Such people legally constitute (if the use of such language is not almost a contradiction in terms) the Church of England congregation and they are empowered at an annual meeting to appoint a parochial church council. The latter, which must meet at least four times in the year, has complete control over the finances of the parish†—and is required to co-operate with the incumbent in the initiation, conduct and development of church work both within the parish and outside. The churchwardens, who are in a sense the incumbent's right-hand men, are appointed (usually) one by the parish priest himself, the other by the vestry meeting,‡ which all ratepayers and members of the electoral roll have the right to attend. The parochial church council is now built into a representative structure within the Church of England which through the ruri-decanal and diocesan conference is linked up with the Church Assembly.

It is perhaps worth noticing that many parochial church councils were called into existence before they became a statutory obligation, since incumbents felt the need to share responsibility with their congregations. Once again the existence of such advisory bodies does not take away from the parish priest the need for leadership: indeed it increases it. He is *ex-officio* chairman of the P.C.C. and a great deal depends on his personal relations with its members and whether he has the

---

* Partially amended by the P.C.C. (Powers) Measure, 1956.

† Except (legally) the offertory at the service of Holy Communion.

‡ This method of appointment of churchwardens is of comparatively recent origin. See Canons of 1603, nos. 89, 90.

skill to make this body responsible. If he is secretly fearful of its deliberations, resentful of its powers, possessive in his attitude and not very expert in handling people, it is unlikely that the P.C.C. will become a very purposeful body. Fortunately most incumbents welcome what they must of necessity put up with, and are glad that corporate responsibility should find expression in this way. They are prepared to take the P.C.C. into their confidence and use it as a sounding board. They gladly consider its ideas, and are happy to benefit from its collective initiative and wisdom. There are many things which members of the P.C.C. can do far better than the incumbent and which are better taken out of his hands so that he may be released for what more properly belongs to him. His overriding concern is that all should bring their contributions to the building of the Kingdom. What he must never do is to think of his P.C.C. as merely in charge of raising money(!) though, of course, the way that such money is raised and spent *does* reflect the priorities which the parish (and the incumbent) think important. Such priorities have a great deal to do with a personal order. Perhaps it may be said here that except for the incumbent's income, which is in the main now received through a grant from the Church Commissioners,* the parish has to be self-supporting, raising by its own efforts the money needed both for its own maintenance and for the wider church—and wider world. It is good that this should be so and that the financial side should not be regarded as faintly obscene, but itself the measure of sacrificial self-giving and a sacramental offering. Indeed, a niggardly and inward-looking parish is not a good reflection of the nature of the Kingdom. Many parishes try to give half their income to extra parochial needs: and all of them have a 'quota' which they are expected to give to the diocese.

The P.C.C., I repeat, is there to work with the incumbent in

* Incomes of incumbents vary but such variations have little to do with the weight of responsibility or size of the parish. Inequalities, however, are becoming less and all dioceses have a minimum net benefice income for incumbents; this varies from diocese to diocese, £850 per annum being a representative figure. The parsonage house is usually held rent and rates free.

directing the total life of the parish. It is a responsible body and the wise parish priest is glad when it is active and vigorous. Indeed it is his ambition to help to make it so and this will often mean breaking down an inherited prejudice which thinks that the parish is really only the parson's concern. The fact, for example, that the organist is appointed by the incumbent but paid by the parochial church council shows how necessary it is that priest and council should work happily together.

As to the character of the church's own community life, this will in the nature of the case vary from parish to parish; and a great deal of experimentation (fortunately) is going on at the present time. Thus all parishes (or nearly all!) have some built-in means of teaching the Faith to young people and for bringing them into the life of the church. On the whole the Sunday school, as traditionally understood, seems to be on the decline and the contemporary tendency is to try to integrate children earlier and more fully into the worshipful life of the church. But Sunday schools, large and small, still flourish in some parishes and with devoted teachers, who (it is hoped) the parish priest or one of his colleagues gets together every week to help and encourage. But whatever be the method—Sunday school, children's church, instruction at the parish communion —it is the continuing concern of the parish priest which will largely determine how far this teaching of the Faith to the young has relevance and is seen to be significant. One thing is quite certain. At a time when teaching is becoming more expert and professional, it is just not good enough in the church to be slipshod and inefficient, though efficiency must never be equated with impersonality. One knows how intimate and enduring the link between Sunday school teacher and scholar can be.

The parish priest will probably regard such instruction given to the young as leading naturally to confirmation, which is the passing on to adult status in the church. At confirmation, the baby, who has now come to 'years of discretion' reaffirms in his own person the promises taken by the god-parents at his baptism. The bishop lays his hands on the head of the young person as he utters the moving prayer: 'Defend, O Lord, this thy child with thy heavenly grace, that he may continue thine for ever; and daily increase in Thy Holy Spirit more and more, until he come unto Thy Everlasting Kingdom.'

In this matter, if I may hazard a personal opinion, the Church of England is hopelessly confused, in that it has linked up an adult dedication to a Christian commitment with a full entry into the worshipful life of the church, through the receiving of the sacrament of Holy Communion. These, in the young, have no necessary connection with each other and often the association prevents families worshipping fully together, unless the adult commitment is entered into at far too young an age. Preparation for confirmation, however, certainly provides the parish priest with a great opportunity, the more so when not entered into too young. It would probably be better for children to come to Communion with their parents perhaps as early as the age of ten, but to defer their adult and responsible commitment to Christian discipleship through confirmation to at least sixteen or eighteen or even older.

In some parishes there will be a church school and the incumbent will be chairman of the managers. He will take a particular interest in its general life, and if he is competent to do so (but only if this is the case—the other teachers might help him here if he is humble enough to learn) he will give instruction in it. Certainly he will get to know the staff and do his best to make the church significant in the school; but at all costs he will remember never to interfere. The head teacher, for all practical purposes, is in charge of the daily running of the school.

Many parochial congregations, under the leadership of the parish priest, undoubtedly experience a great sense of fellowship and become purposeful communities. Personal relations are intimate and satisfying and they overflow into all kinds of activities of which it is enough merely to suggest a few— discussion groups, 'cells' for prayer, dramatic societies, dancing and sports clubs. For young people there may be Scouts, Guides, Church Lads Brigade, and Youth Fellowships. Then there are such long established institutions as the Mothers' Union and the Church of England Men's Society. Some parishes lay on a group summer holiday. All these add to vitality and enable people to confront and meet each other. It is not, of course, the 'job' of the incumbent to run these, even if this were physically possible, but it is his responsibility to see the need for such a coming together, and to give friendship and help to those lay people who undertake this care. The 'leader' will often wish to talk things over with him; and anyhow in an essentially personal society the parish priest will be the representative through whom the groups will know that they are members one of another. This is a priestly task. It is easy for a club leader to feel isolated, ploughing a lonely furrow, out on a limb: it is the parish priest's responsibility to deal with this psychological frustration before it happens. Also it is a good thing for the priest on behalf of the parish, to say 'Thank you' from time to time. Most of us are encouraged by a little appreciation.

Not all parishes, of course, necessarily lean to or demand a variety of organisations. Certainly they grow naturally out of the soil of suburbia—but not everywhere. There is, possibly, still a difference here between town and country. The knowledgeable parish priest understands his local situation.

To repeat. The incumbent who, except in special circumstances, get himself bogged down in running everything is not serving his community to the best advantage, nor is he really making his own specific contribution. He needs to encourage his lay people to be responsible and to be fellow-workers with him. Indeed, he might well establish teams of laymen. What is important is that he, as the parish priest, should have a sustained and active concern. He must recognise that activities centred around the church help to make a congregation into a community by exposing the members to one another. A personal order needs to realise itself through immediate encounter, and the social life of the church ought not to be seen as a kind of light relief, the carrot which, dangled before the eyes of the donkey, persuades it reluctantly to go forward. Rather it should be regarded as the necessary overflow of a worship which is social in character. Religion is relationship. A Christ-committed life needs to embody itself in a mutual sharing and concern. The worshipper is not an isolated unit making a lonely offering, but the highly particular member of a living community. And this community reaches out beyond itself through diocese and province into the wider world of the universal church. There are many ways ('Our Own Missionary' for example) in which this universality can be brought home to the local community. Ultimately it is a matter of 'feel', of awareness, of approach. The parish priest sees his own church and congregation in this broad context. It gives him a sense of perspective and prevents any inward-looking view.

Such a social life fostered around the church first began, undoubtedly, as a service to the community, and a means of evangelism at a time before there were any such amenities laid on by other agencies, whether local authorities or national organisations. Reference has already been made, in this respect, to thrift clubs, penny readings and the heroic labours of the slum parson. Times have changed considerably since those days and church activities no longer stand alone, nor would they, for the most part, now be regarded as 'remedial', as once was the case. Rather their concern is to foster a living spirit of fellowship within a particular community, though this will splinter off into a wider dimension. Local authorities are usually able to provide far better facilities, and keen Christians will often be found working within such services. Yet this does not mean that there is no place for clubs geared to or arising out of a Christian commitment, and 'run' by a voluntary personnel.

Yet over and above this, it will always remain necessary that the members of a worshipping community should become 'known' to each other so that they really can grow into a real family. For such to happen they need to become involved and caught up in a common life.

In trying to make an effective society out of those gathered into his parish church, the parish priest will not be unaware in his own neighbourhood of other Christian communities, Roman Catholics, Free Churches, Quakers, indeed of any group seeking to realise a personal order. Here he is in a unique position to show initiative, the more so since his representative capacity means that he brings his community with him as he penetrates into the structure of the local life. At a time when there is a significant coming together of churches, the parish priest can help to translate this movement into concrete terms in his own neighbourhood. It is easier for him, in the first instance, to do something about this than for anyone else, though the Council of Churches may sponsor and encourage activities in a larger area. The parish priest will be quick to appreciate the integrity of other religious groups and their place in the total community life around him, the more so as the Church of England is itself 'comprehensive' and as such is not wholly alien to any of them. To encroach, to resent, or to endeavour to interfere with them will never be his intention. Religious controversy is usually the most sterile of all human exercises and we may safely assume that the occasions are rare indeed when the parish priest ought to feel that he must protect his flock from crudely false assertions. On the whole such protective activities are not to be encouraged. The accepted status of the parish priest, however, does mean that his initiative in the matter of bringing churches together, if sensitively and not brashly taken, is less likely to be misunderstood than a similar initiative taken by anyone else, particularly when the parish priest's concern is known to spring, not from a desire to gain converts for his own group, but from a passion to build with others the Kingdom of God.

Once again everything depends on the character of the priest, on the largeness of his vision, his liberality and maturity. The insecure man will not find it easy to take the right initiative, and the non-sensitive man will not always know that there is any initiative which can be taken. But the opportunity is there, and it is good that there should be one person in a favourable position to take it.

H

CHAPTER 7

THE WIDER COMMUNITY

IT is now necessary to turn to the position of the parish priest in relation to the local community as a whole, to his overall and diffused responsibility.

Here, of course, and I must say this again at the risk of some wearisome repetition, everything, or nearly everything, will depend on his own ability and concern. He *can* play a significant rôle in the affairs of his neighbourhood, but only if he is adequate to take it. He must be willing to serve. He may, of course, be required to hold certain positions *ex officio* (for example to be a school manager) but even here his real influence will largely depend on how acceptable he is as a person, in particular whether he evokes confidence, is active, and seems to care.

Not only, however, will he wish to involve himself, in a representative capacity, in this wider society, but he will also encourage his own congregation to serve it in all that relates to the corporate life, whether this be in relation to municipal government, road safety, social amenities, U.N.A., famine relief, education in schools, and so on. Without weakening the solidarity of the home base, the incumbent will have a sense of the neighbourhood, and the needs of all its residents of whom he is one. He will not so limit the implications of the word 'religion' as to feel that his 'secular' activities are alien to his Christian commitment. Indeed he and his congregation may themselves well learn something as to the nature of God's Kingdom from dedicated people who make no profession of religious faith, but who labour to build in season and out of season a personal order in which their fellow men can find a home. The Christian gives to the world, but he also receives from it, and any suggestion of condescension or a 'holier than thou' attitude is as repulsive as it is inappropriate. If the parish priest is leading an outward-looking society, and it is his job to see that his congregation is so, then he himself is more likely to be trusted as he goes out to meet and share responsibility in the place where he lives.

What has been said earlier in respect of relations with other churches obtains equally in this context. The parish priest can often provide an initiative which it is not so easy for others to take and which comes less embarrassingly from himself. Sometimes, for example, he may be asked to convene a special meeting, to start a branch of U.N.A. (this happened to me) or a choral society, to revive a village football club, to appeal for blood donors. I know a parish priest who called together a council to foster better race relations in his area. Instances could be added almost *ad infinitum*. He is in a position to win support for a good cause and to associate others with him. Sometimes he himself is in a unique position to sense a need and to do something positive about it.

But he must not always expect to play the leading rôle, or to be the *fons et origo bonorum*. It will be good for him, and helpful to his parish, if he is content to work diligently with other people though he is not in the forefront, perhaps serving as a member of an education committee or indeed of a local authority itself. What he must never do is to accept office and then be a passenger.

This all adds up to saying that the parish priest ought, when circumstances allow, to be a local figure, whose activities are seen to be by no means confined to his own flock. This outward look should be equally characteristic of the community he leads. It may well be that on occasions, when anyone asks whether he might undertake 'church work', the appropriate reply would be to suggest putting up for election on the local council. If the parish priest is always self-consciously asking himself in respect of every activity what return this is likely to have on church membership, he will frustrate himself and betray that he has little first-hand knowledge of living in the Kingdom. The Kingdom is not so clearly defined. A great deal of the world (in the bad sense of the word) is in the church, and a great deal of the Kingdom in the world—and *vice versa*. That the vicar can become significant in his local community there is no doubt whatever. Many have become so. The present Bishop of

Southwark served on the local authority when he was an incumbent in Bristol. Even in the sixties there is enough of a historic hangover and residual good-will for him to come in on; but he will only come in on it if he has the capacity to do so and has something positive to offer. Indeed it might well be claimed that in the modern welfare state, so all-embracing and complex in its structure, there is even more need for the person who can introduce into its corporate existence particular personal categories, and see the total situation steadily and see it whole.

In industrial areas where the priest finds it tough and hard going, and often difficult to gather an active (or even any) congregation around him, it may well be that his initial approach will be to identify himself with the wider community and its more general needs. In this way he can witness to and build the Kingdom, while he works patiently to foster the growth of a dedicated society around the name of Christ. In large city communities he will seek to play his part in municipal affairs, and make contact with the Mayor and Corporation.

The penetration of the priest, and the community he leads, into the wider society around him is thus twofold.

It is at one level personal: at another it is what may loosely be described as structural, since its concern is with local group interests. A neighbourhood is not simply an atomistic conglomeration of unrelated units. There are structures within it which are powerfully formative in the life of the community—schools, trade unions, chambers of commerce, hospitals—even the local football club. The parish priest must be aware of these and where possible identify himself and what he stands for with them. He will try to get to know, and maybe make friends with representative people such as schoolmasters, doctors, employers, trade unionists, with his member of Parliament—indeed all those who occupy key positions around him.

From what has been said so far in this chapter, it might, perhaps, be thought that the parish priest is a jack of all trades and a master of none; that he dabbles in everything. The criticism has point in so far as it refers to the fact that whatever his abilities and aptitudes, they are directed towards the welfare of persons within the context of their full life. In this respect the parish priest must be a good all-rounder. His excellency comes from the unity that he imposes upon a wide area of personal and group experience. Of course he has his expertise. He needs to know how to order public worship. He must be theologically informed generally and with a good biblical knowledge in particular. He needs to cultivate an interior life which has range and depth since one of his duties is to pray regularly for his people and to lead them in prayer. This demands great self-discipline.

But this expertise, I repeat, is introduced into a community life in which a care for persons is paramount: and this introduction demands a non-doctrinaire approach, a universality of interests, infinite resource and the ability to size up a situation when it comes. All the manuals in the world, unfortunately, will not provide answers to most of the problems which come the way of the parish priest. It is *nous*, insight, the capacity to learn from experience, sheer horse sense which matter. The parish priest cannot avoid making snap decisions, and living with the result of them. He must not, therefore, be afraid of accepting responsibility. The community through which he works (unlike a cathedral staff) is for the most part voluntary, and he must be able to keep it purposefully together. To 'get on' with people is at least 75 per cent of his 'job'.

Such a statement of ambition may well prompt the question: 'Who is sufficient for these things?' and lead to the conclusion that it might be better to make the parish priest a much more specialised person altogether. For myself I doubt this, though this is not to say that there is no room for more specialised persons within the ministry of the Church of England. There most certainly is, as I shall suggest later. What I am insisting upon, however, is that the peculiar merit of the parish priest lies in the fact that he touches life at many points; and that it is just this multiplicity of approach which enriches his ministry and gives him his unique flair. It can make him effective in the place where he is. There is (in my judgment) everything to be said for the man who leads the worship himself visiting the sick, giving pastoral help, wrestling with the intellectual doubts of his flock, leading a diverse community, seeing that piano A is transported from room B to hall C, and being involved in the life of his own family. This serves to make him a rounded person and thereby capable of ministering to people in the wholeness of their immediate situation. It gives a particular 'flavour' to any one task that he undertakes. What he must know, like a good G.P., is when to call in the expert, when for example this intellectual doubt needs more profound elucidation, or that anxiety demands a trained psychiatrist.

He must also remember that laymen are quite properly impatient with inefficiency—inefficiency of a kind which in their own line of country would bankrupt a business in a twelve-month—and with equal propriety they have little time for laziness. There is everything to be said for answering letters and starting meetings and services on time!

In this respect, however, it needs to be said—that a parish priest cannot possibly have too set or rigid a time-table. Sudden death, and the needs of his parishioners generally, will not oblige by fitting into his diary, and like a doctor he must make himself available to meet emergent situations when they happen. In a very real sense he does not know, when he gets up in the morning, what the day will bring forth. This uncertainty, however, makes it even more necessary that there should be great self-discipline; and that he should make the most of the odd quarter of an hour between engagements. It can be used for invaluable reading. There is no profession in which it is easier to waste time pottering about the house!

I myself believe that in an age of increasing specialisation in which there is at least some element of truth in the jibe that more and more is known of less and less, there is abundant room for the general practitioner, the man who (paradoxically) becomes a specialist through his specialisation on the whole; through his having no one isolated expertise. The clergyman has a particular line of country, of course—he is a priest—but in his line of country it is the need to bring together unique people into a personal order which constitutes the immediate and indeed the distant scene. It is surely inconceivable that in our contemporary age, with its focal points of interest too often on the circumference rather than in the centre, there is neither place nor need for a cultivated person, committed to a great Faith, who puts himself at the disposal of his local community, and is released from other pursuits for this single purpose.

This is another way of saying that the clergyman's rôle is a dual one. Though involved in, and sharing the day-to-day existence of his parishioners, he ought to be able to stand outside some of the disruptions which break up local communities. He has no personal axe to grind; no vested interest whatever except to build a personal order to the advantage of everybody. Most people's work necessarily lies in a specialised field: he deals with the whole. The schoolmaster, the barrister, the factory worker, the shop-keeper, these all have relations with people, but with people in particular and highly specialised contexts. The priest is asked to weep with those who weep and rejoice with those who rejoice. He goes from a baptism, to a marriage, to a funeral. His judgment has value (when it has!) because it arises out of a wide experience of men and affairs and at the same time is set within the context of a Faith which gives unique dignity to persons.

It has been said of the parish priest, that in the best sense he is a gifted amateur. Such a statement is liable to be misunderstood, but there is certainly an element (but only an element) of truth in it. His 'job' cannot be reduced to rule of thumb, and though there are many excellent books which teach him what every clergyman ought to know—how he should arrange his day, and conduct his business—in the end he finds that it is a general sensitivity together with an awareness of present needs which stands him in greatest stead.

If a man, stepping into the inheritance and 'plant' of the parish priest (no matter how whittled away the inheritance is) and entrusted with the responsibilities which he undertakes cannot contribute uniquely to the life of the community around him, then, I suspect, something is wrong with *him*. Such failure is more likely to happen if he sees his priest-like task too narrowly and affects to despise 'serving tables'. His is a sacrificial priesthood in the fullest sense of the word. True many of the social duties that town and country parsons used to discharge are now done more adequately by local authorities: but this by no means takes away from the significance of the local clergyman. It can leave him greater scope in papering over the cracks, and introducing the personal categories for which he stands into the vast complex of modern life. He may be more needed than ever in a technological age: and the local Christian community within which he 'lives and moves and has his being' will not lack a contemporary task.

Being a parish priest is a tough job. It can be physically exhausting: it makes great demands on a man's nervous resources and imposes upon him a need for rigid self-discipline. But it is a 'whole' and many-sided job. In some rural areas it gives him the priceless gift of a leisure which can be of enormous benefit to his community, but which if abused can become corrupting to him as a person. To the man of resource the parochial priesthood is uniquely satisfying, in spite of the frustrations and disappointments which it must be admitted many men experience, particularly if they are working within the industrial scene. The parish priest may sometimes feel that he is handicapped by the conservatism of the church as an institution, its timidity, its remoteness from modern secular society and often its devastating respectability. At other times he may think that the intellectual assents demanded of him pose problems of conscience which it is not always easy to solve. Yet within the tension that this creates—for in the nature of the case there must always be tension between the individual and the group—there will come the assurance that he is engaged on a task which requires and deserves an absolute committal, for the task is none other than to build the Kingdom of God. It is, in the main, through him that the theology of Christian Faith becomes meaningful to ordinary people. He may, humbly, be persuaded that through his dedication life can flow back into the church. Certainly to be in charge of a parish is the most responsible, certainly the most exacting and difficult task which the Church of England entrusts to its ordained ministers. It is ironic that all too often many good priests are taken out of their parishes and projected into posts of greater dignity which men with far less all round ability could perform equally well—if not better.

CHAPTER 8

CATHEDRAL AND BISHOP

THE incumbent works in a parish and the parish looks out immediately to the rural deanery, which is presided over by a rural dean appointed by the bishop.* The clergy of such an area meet from time to time to discuss common problems, and it is in this way that the parish is linked up with the diocese. The rural dean has a responsible position and can prove helpful to his brother parish priests if he is that kind of person. From time to time he holds a visitation.

A number of rural deaneries form an archdeaconry, which in its turn is presided over by an archdeacon usually appointed by the bishop. In the Middle Ages the archdeacon had his own very effective court, and since it had jurisdiction over matters of intimate concern to many families (wills, for example) he was frequently an object of vilification, and it was a moot point as to whether an archdeacon could be saved. To-day a more kindly view is taken of him. There is perhaps little point in listing his duties except in so far as they illustrate in general the nature of his office. Typical is his visitation, which is usually held (unfortunately not in the parish) after Easter when the church-wardens make their presentments, and the archdeacon discusses with them the state of their parish, including the upkeep and condition of the church. Generally it is his duty to inspect and reform abuses among the clergy, to present candidates for ordination, to induct to benefices, to admit churchwardens, and to preside over extraordinary meetings of the parochial church council, made necessary when there is trouble in a parish involving the incumbent. The archdeacon, as is natural in view of his administrative functions, sits on the diocesan conference in addition to many committees and boards of patronage, and

* In many dioceses the bishop asks the clergy of the rural deanery to make suggestions.

often he is a member of the Lower House of Convocation and the Church Assembly. It is clear that the office demands administrative ability, but this makes it even more necessary that the archdeacon should be alive to pastoral and parochial needs and blessed with a great understanding of people. If he lacks these endowments his efficiency will not in practice add up to very much. It is not unusual for some archdeacons to hold a small living and there is a great deal to be said for this. He is thereby constantly reminded of what he administers.

A number of archdeaconries makes up a diocese and it is over the diocese that the bishop presides.* Before, however, indicating briefly the nature of the bishop's office, it will be helpful to look at the cathedral, which is the chief church of the diocese and where the bishop has his *cathedra* or throne.

Most cathedrals are ancient buildings and it is clear that our ancestors lavished a vast capital expenditure upon them. England is fortunate in that it possesses so many, and for the most part in so fine a state of preservation. Only four cathedrals have been built since the Reformation, namely Truro, Liverpool, Guildford and Coventry. The governing body of a cathedral is the dean and chapter, usually some five clergymen, with the bishop as visitor: and its constitution, revised many times since, usually goes back to the sixteenth century when cathedrals were drastically changed in their corporate life as a result of the Reformation. The function of the clergy attached to a cathedral is to order the daily worship, to engage in serious scholarship, to make the cathedral a focal point for the life of the diocese and of course to maintain and beautify the building.

It has to be admitted that the older cathedrals were not designed for congregational worship or for some of the uses to which they are now put. The choir is often enclosed, which is admirably suited to the daily recital of their 'offices' by monastic or secular clergy: but because of this the great diocesan services which take place in cathedrals present problems, particularly if the worship is non-liturgical in form. For this reason they are

* There are 43 dioceses in England—29 in the province of Canterbury, and 14 in the province of York.

often held in the nave. Preaching in such buildings is difficult though microphones have made audibility possible as never before. Yet in spite of their handicaps a determined effort is increasingly being made to link up the cathedral with the life of the parishes, and to encourage an easy movement between the one and the other.

The responsibility for the upkeep of such buildings is no sinecure, for it represents a constant fight against the ravages of time. Indeed their preservation is in one sense an unnatural exercise, for nearly all domestic buildings of the same period have disappeared. Constant vigilance, a steady expenditure of money with occasional large capital sums are absolutely necessary. The cathedrals receive no state aid but are largely dependent upon grants from the Church Commissioners, from the diocese, from the offerings of visitors and gifts maybe from the Historic Churches Preservation Trust. Periodic appeals are necessary but it is questionable how far such a constant preoccupation with money is a good thing or helps the dean and chapter to discharge their wider responsibilities. Yet these buildings are a priceless heritage and themselves represent an act of worship in stone. They still inspire. But it is a pity if the cathedral clergy are thought of primarily as custodians of an ancient building, though this responsibility is of course important. In discharging their duties the dean and chapter are helped by expert lay advisors who take a heavy load off their shoulders, but under the terms of their constitution final responsibility rests with the clergy as a governing body.

The clergy at a cathedral are expected to have a particular line of country in which they are reasonably expert. It does not unfortunately always work out like this in practice. Sometimes an excellent parish priest is appointed to a cathedral post for which his gifts and abilities, invaluable where he was, do not fit him. This is more likely to happen when a false view is taken of preferment. The result is frustration for everyone concerned. Historically deans and chapters have often been somewhat unhappy bodies prone to internal division. Many men, after having run their own parishes for a number of years, find it difficult to settle down as members of a team in which the pace is geared down to the slowest vessel in the convoy (and how slow some of them can be! When they move, it is often in a reverse direction!).

This is why it is important that the canons should have a particular flair, a specialised interest, an enthusiasm, a personal concern. For them a cathedral can provide a unique opportunity. A man with a lively ecumenical or liturgical interest would find the cathedral a good centre from which to operate, if the bishop and dean and chapter are co-operative. It is a good thing when one of the cathedral clergy has a marked social conscience. All of them ought to have something of significance to say in the pulpit. Sometimes a canon has a diocesan appointment, which is useful when it serves to associate the cathedral with the wider life of the church around: but it is bad when resorted to merely as a means of saving money, and as a consequence burdens the cathedral with an unsuitable person. A cathedral also provides an excellent base for a scholar, which is important at a time when the teaching responsibilities of many university dons give them less and less leisure for serious research. The Church of England desperately needs men who are prepared to give their minds to the understanding and elucidation of Christian Faith within the context of the contemporary world. A balanced religious society needs 'back-room boys' engaged in specialised study and the cathedrals ought to be able to provide them. It is almost certainly the case that many people are indifferent to Christian Faith simply because they do not basically believe it to be true. There is an overriding need at the present time, consequent upon the flooding in of so much new knowledge and in a changed climate of thought, to build up a coherent intellectual rationale.

Once again, I am suggesting in a new context what I have already called attention to earlier. The cathedral, in spite of many unresolved problems of contemporary deployment, can become really significant in itself, and in the use to which it is put. It is, of course, and must remain, a place for the sightseer to visit, and if imaginatively looked after it will continue to speak eloquently in such brief encounters. A cathedral which suggests both tradition and contemporaneity will interest in a unique way. True, many such buildings are aesthetically disfigured by vast collections of statuary; but even here it is better, since they exist, to make the most of them, to see that they are clean and where appropriate, given colour. In some odd way they may even serve to associate the common life of man in its law, its politics, its government with the claims of the Kingdom of God. Certainly clergy at cathedral institutions need to eschew the kind of preciousness which removes them too far from this solid earth, though they ought, within a rhythm of worship, to introduce into earthiness another and more transcendental reference. Released as they are from a pastoral oversight, they have a duty to the diocese, and above and beyond this to the church and nation as a whole. They need imagination, energy (in their own field) and the capacity to persevere with their interest.

The dean, who is the head and presides over meetings of chapter, can make a most valuable contribution to the life of a city if he has the ability, drive and enthusiasm to come in on it in the right way. Together with two of the archdeacons from the diocese, he is usually an *ex officio* member of both Church Assembly and Convocation and thus has a voice in the wider life of the church. The cathedral can also provide a good centre for the arts, for musical recitals, for exhibitions, for lectures and the challenging presentation of a full faith—and this at a high level.

Cathedral cities with their mayor and corporation, their hospitals, their colleges and schools, their prisons, their cultural activities, embody a rich variety of human encounter. The cathedral can become meaningful here but it must not be taken for granted that this will necessarily happen, unless there is the dynamic and imagination to make it happen. The cathedral must be seen to stand for something, as, for example, at Coventry. Too many such societies still succeed in sleeping peacefully, their little life being self-contained, cosy and comfortable. What would not the dedicated communist give for such built-in opportunities as these institutions provide?

The head of the diocese is the bishop, who is appointed by the Crown, as is the case with deans and often with canons. Such appointments come *via* the Prime Minister, who through his appointments secretary, or personally, seeks advice as widely as he can, both clerical and lay, including, of course, from the Archbishop of Canterbury, and, if the vacancy is in the northern province, from the Archbishop of York.

It would be a digression in this book to discuss at length the relative merits and demerits of this manner of appointment, concerning which an Archbishop's Commission is soon to report.* The method goes back, in its present ambiguous form, to the Middle Ages, when little distinction was made between church and state and the bishops were important figures in the life of the nation, holding great offices at court. Thus the Crown had an interest in their appointment and the usual practice was for it to enter into an agreement with the Papacy in order to secure its own nominees. In the nineteenth century both the Crown and the Prime Minister took a great personal interest in the choosing of bishops and regarded this as a weighty responsibility.

Those who, in the main, support the present system (though wishing to reform it in certain respects and make it work more effectively) maintain that in practice it leads to a greater variety of gifts on the episcopate, avoids, over against election, unsuccessful candidates, and in the given historical situation secures a lay interest thereby preventing ecclesiastical introversion. It also charges the senior minister of state with a heavy responsibility toward, and therefore a built-in interest in, the well-being of the Church of England. It represents, in this respect, Establishment.

Such arguments are, of course, entirely pragmatic in character: and most of those who oppose this method of selection see it as wrong in principle, since they maintain that the church should choose its own bishop by its own methods and through its own membership, maybe by some form of electoral college. It needs to be remembered, of course, that under the present system, though the Crown nominates the bishop to a particular diocese or suffragan see, only the church in a narrower sense can consecrate him by the laying on of

* This was written on October 2, 1964.

hands to this order in the threefold ministry. The church has the final responsibility.

The office of a bishop has been with the church since very early days, and many would see him as a successor of the Apostles, and as such representing a necessary order through which God confers grace to the various ministries within his church. In this sense he is essential to its very existence. Not all Anglicans, since the Reformation, however, would take such a high or extreme view. Some see the bishop, not as essential to the life of the church, but as an ancient and valuable ingredient within it, guaranteeing continuity, preventing proliferation, and bearing witness to a stable order. As such the bishop has traditionally been associated with the maintenance of right doctrine —i.e. Christian truth.

The fact is that varying views as to the nature of the episcopate exist side by side within the Church of Englancd.

The special functions which the bishop discharges may be briefly summarised. It is the bishop who ordains priests and makes deacons, confirms the baptised, consecrates and invests bishops. He licenses incumbents to benefices and also assistant curates and has a pastoral oversight over all the clergy of his diocese. The bishops sit together in the Upper House of Convocation which they constitute, and they preside over their diocesan conference (where they have a power of veto). They have seats in the Church Assembly and are usually *ex officio* members of numerous (far too numerous) committees.

The bishop's first care is a pastoral one to his own clergy, to whom, in the words of the Order of Consecration in the Book of Common Prayer, he is required to be a 'shepherd'. At every institution of a parish priest the bishop says: 'Receive the cure of souls which is both yours and mine.' To become a real 'Father in God' means entering into personal relations, making himself available, and supporting his clergy in every way. This is an aspect of his work which no mere brilliance of parts can achieve. It is a matter of basic human understanding, being willing to give time (sometimes of seeming to waste time), winning confidence, and becoming sensitive to particular situations. Clergy often need encouragement in loneliness, advice and friendship: the bishop can be invaluable in bringing these to them. By and large, however, the clergy will resort to him for help and guidance only if he is the sort of person whom they feel they can trust and who understands them. There are certainly occasions when a bishop has to be tough, but this toughness will only secure its real end if he is first known as a friend and the seeming toughness is recognised as an expression of a deep pastoral concern. On many matters the clergy are, according to resolutions of Convocation and the Church Assembly, embodied in diocesan regulations, required to consult their bishop (i.e. on admission of divorced persons to Communion, the holding of a service in church after a marriage in a registrar's office; the inviting a Free Churchman to preach etc.). Here a wise bishop will encourage his clergy to make responsible decisions themselves and to live with the results of them. Such necessary consultations, however, do give the bishop an opportunity of making a personal contact. The more developed of his clergy will probably not trouble him very much in matters of parochial routine, nor he them, for it is important that nothing be done which takes away from the parish priest the burden of personal decision. He must not become merely an official, an agent, the instrument through which a policy is implemented. One of the least happy features of the contemporary situation is the tendency of too many younger clergy to wish to have their orders. Yet in spite of this, it is still true that the Anglican ministry is often the last resort of the individualist—a fact which makes nonsense of the so-called 'shackles of the Establishment'. It is this very Establishment which safeguards such freedom. The parish priest would doubtless try to carry on even if some cosmic catastrophe deprived him of both cathedral and bishop.

Though the bishop's primary responsibility is towards his own clergy, it by no means ends there. The fact that he goes round his diocese means that he can become known to parishioners generally. He comes in on the life of a parochial community at some of its most significant moments, for example at the institution of a new incumbent, at confirmation, the celebration of centenaries and so on. As these encounters are in their nature brief, it is important that the bishop should have the kind of personality which comes alive in this somewhat hurried context. Leadership defies explanation, but it is none-theless a very real thing. Certainly the influence of the bishop in his diocese is often subtly formative. He can become a rallying point for its common life. He can create a general feeling that the church means business, that it has a cutting edge, and that in the best sense it is contemporary and seeking to be relevant. By touching the life of the diocese at so many points, religious, social and educational, he is able to give a total direction. Doubtless he is asked to do so many things that it is often difficult for him to decide upon priorities. The temptation will be to become far too busy and to run dry. If he succumbs this can become painfully evident, not least when he gets up to speak. Priorities, of course, must largely be determined by the nature of his office, the character of the diocese, and the particular gifts of the person concerned. There are occasions when it is better not to do something than to do this something badly, though such occasions are rare!

The bishop, however, is not only a diocesan figure, and it is his additional responsibilities which are one of the reasons why he is usually helped by suffragans. He has an extra-diocesan significance both in relation to the Church of England as a whole and historically to the life of the nation.

The bishop is a representative person and through him the diocese is linked up with the province and more widely with the church universal. He is a member of the Church Assembly and sits in the Upper House of Convocation, and this necessarily means that he ought to be theologically informed, a man of a shrewd and penetrating judgment. As a diocesan bishop he attends the Lambeth Conference, normally held every ten years, at which bishops from all over the Anglican Communion are present. He will receive invitations to go on American tours, to visit Australia, and on all these peregrinations he will be seen as somehow embodying the ethos and the general feel of the Church of England.

But the bishop is not only an important ecclesiastical figure. Through his unique place in English history, he is something more. True sometimes this additional status may be an embarrassment since it can tend to create a false and antiquarian image, suggestive of a museum piece. It is a fact, however, that the bishop has loomed large in our island story, in particular, the Archbishop of Canterbury who crowns the sovereign. Indeed Archbishop Laud was felt to be so important, in the middle years of the seventeenth century, that Parliament executed him. The bishops have been used governmentally and in the eighteenth century their lobby in the House of Lords was of great significance. Thus political motives often dominated episcopal appointments. Still to-day what a bishop says is regarded as news: he is a national figure. His support for a good cause is eagerly sought after. He is still regarded by laymen as in a very special sense representing the church—a fact which perhaps naturally tends to make many bishops overcautious and somewhat chary of speaking their mind.

Some bishops sit in the House of Lords by virtue of the see that they hold, others because of seniority. Such a responsible privilege undoubtedly presents a problem, in part a problem of time. The occasional intruder into the Upper House, as is the case with the backwoodsman who descends upon it only when questions of vested interests are concerned, never becomes sensitive to its ethos and he is at a disadvantage when he really wants to commend a point of view. Also it is difficult to make a distinction between the sacred and the secular, and many would maintain that it is theologically improper even to attempt to do so. Certainly it would be quite disastrous if the bishops only made their voices heard on so-called religious matters or contemporary moral problems. The idea of one of them keeping a watching brief is not very pleasant though it may be the best that can be done in the circumstances. The Christian is concerned with the whole life of the nation, and in particular with the lifting up of its affairs into a more truly personal order. As such it is not enough simply to intervene in discussions on Premium Bonds, or new divorce legislation. Episcopal representation in the Lords is a historical legacy from a day and generation when the bishop was more significant politically and held a somewhat different view of his office. In the eighteenth century he would normally expect to live in

London for part of the year simply in order to attend the Court and his Parliamentary duties. His successor is caught up in a multiplicity of engagements in his own diocese; and he very properly takes far more seriously his pastoral responsibility *vis-à-vis* his own clergy. It is just not easy to fit attendance in the House of Lords into this programme.

Also it is probably true to say that most bishops would not see themselves as suited to contribute much in an assembly of this kind, nor are most of them sufficiently informed politically to be able to speak with ease, authority and information. Indeed they might well regard certain political debates as too divisive for them to join in. On the other hand the nature of their office does mean that they touch life at many points and this could well give weight to their testimony. Certain bishops do, I believe, try to attend when their own particular line of interest is involved; but it must be admitted that the episcopal representation in the House of Lords is not so significant as it used or ought to be. Some might argue that a representation arising out of a past history is best preserved by making it unobtrusive and not too evident: but the wisdom and indeed rightness of this attitude may well be questioned. The justification of the continued presence of the bishops can only be that they make a positive contribution to the total life of the nation.* Such representation should therefore be made a meaningful and present reality. To suggest this is, of course, no criticism of the bishops, but a commentary on a system which exposes them to conflicting duties and responsibilities.

It was, I think, Troeltsch who insisted that it is a part of the function of a great church, not simply to inspire individual people, but to enter into relationships with groups and social structures. The bishop, as himself the expression of an order, is in a unique position to do this and he is a natural focus around which it can be done. He stands for the penetration of the Gospel, not only into the home but into the wider life of the nation. An episcopate with a cutting edge, standing significantly

* It would be a good thing if the Church of England took the appropriate initiative in suggesting some form of representation from other religious denominations.

for social righteousness, would help the parish priest by making the church seem more meaningful to ordinary and often non-church-going parishioners. It is the business of the bishop to commend the personal order for which Christianity stands in the seats of power. The emphasis now placed on the bishop's vocation as a pastor, in distinction from the time when Wesley said that a bishop to him was a wig and lawn sleeves, is right and proper: but it would be a pity for the bishop not to be thought of as something more, as carrying the church along with him into the collective and national life. The point is a subtle one, but at a time when the nation tends more and more to throw up group loyalties within itself it is important for the church to do two things: first to insist on the priority of personal encounter, and secondly to recognise the integrity of the structures in which such encounters take place. It is the bishop's particular concern to see that the church's order penetrates into the collective group life—as, for example, into the trade unions, the Federation of British Industries—much of which has developed its own *esprit de corps*, and as a consequence can be corporately suggestible or resistant to the influence of the church. Here is something of which the bishop, and not only he, must be conscious.

The fact that there are still Assize Sermons; that there is a chaplain to the Speaker of the House of Commons; and that the day's business begins with prayer is not without significance.

Outside the diocesan pattern of the Church of England are the royal peculiars of Westminster Abbey and St. George's Chapel, Windsor. These institutions are exempt from episcopal and archi-episcopal jurisdiction. The sovereign is the Visitor and appoints the personnel of the Dean and Chapter. The clergy who serve these royal peculiars have a great opportunity to develop along an individual line and to show a real initiative. Their independence ought to be capable of being made meaningful at a time when, as the 'winds of change' blow, bold experimentation is needed in the church. They betray a trust if they are not creatively pioneering.

CHAPTER 9

SPECIALISED MINISTRIES

So far I have been talking in a general way of the parish priest in his own locality, of the cathedral clergy and the bishop. I have stressed the significance of residence and the overall and many-sided nature of the parish priest's responsibilities. His writ is a wide one, but it would be absurd, of course, to assume that the parochial ministry is to-day capable, on its own, of undertaking the vast and bold duty of proclaiming and witnessing to the Kingdom. It represents, I believe, the most normative and probably the most stable means of engaging in this task, and will probably remain so. That it will be submitted to some changes in the next few years is, I suspect, certain, but in its essence it is likely to persist for a very long time.

But by no means all clergy are parish priests, even among those who accept a pastoral responsibility, and it is about these that I now wish briefly to speak. The nature of their work is more specialised and they are themselves more specialised people. It would be a pity if what follows seems a mere catalogue: but certain things must be said since this book is in part a documentary.

Every hospital has its chaplain appointed by its Management Committee and Board of Governors under the National Health Service Act of 1949. The Anglican chaplain may be full or part-time according to the number of beds. He has a pastoral responsibility for all who in any way describe themselves as 'Church of England'; but in practice, of course, his task and the people to whom he ministers cannot be limited in this way. He has an opportunity of becoming a 'person' in the hospital and introducing himself into its life and interests.

The chaplain visits patients, administers the sacraments, conducts ward or chapel services, and endeavours to become a friend to everybody. He ministers also to the staff and, if there are any, to the medical students. Once again, and how monotonous this is beginning to sound, whether he can come in on his status and privileged position depends on the sort of person he is. If he forgets what is his primary task, is of the interfering kind, tends to look out for snubs, and is insensitive to the hospital routine, then he will find that opportunities for service diminish. But if he remembers never to be in the way and never out of the way, to be easily accessible, to show initiative at the right time, and is prepared to enter into the total community life of the hospital, he will find it possible to translate his office into a living reality.

The full time chaplain, in ministering in the main to the sick, will inevitably acquire a specialised skill. But the acquirement of this expertise has corresponding dangers. All people are not sick (at least physically!) and to the patients the hospital is no abiding city. True it is an intense little world while it lasts but their interests remain primarily outside it. Sometimes it is more abiding to the chaplain. This makes it imperative that he should enter into the general life of the hospital, keep up with his personal friends and the wider church outside, in order that he may remain a rounded person. Also by so doing he becomes aware of the difficulties which, in the nature of the case, beset the staff, whether they be the young nurse, the medical student, the surgeon, and indeed a vast range of other workers upon whose co-operation the running of the hospital necessarily depends.

Here again it is a matter of right relations and the ability to make them. Particularly the chaplain must be the kind of person who can work with a predominantly female staff. The matron, in the nature of the case, is the most significant person in a hospital. She (as well as others) is likely to consult the chaplain if she has come to know him as a person and is impressed with his insight, commonsense and integrity. The fact that he is a priest may provoke the desire to see him in the first place; but whether this leads to subsequent meetings depends on an assessment of the chaplain as a person. The value of the chaplain's getting to know people in a general way is that it makes it easier for them to call upon him for help when they are in need.

The parish priest, operating in the smaller hospital, is not, of course, a specialist in quite the same way, but what he lacks in this direction can in part be compensated for by the knowledge gained in a more balanced society. Also he has a community behind him which can be of help in this ministry. It ought to be said that the full-time chaplain is exposed to exceptional strain. He has the advantage of always being around, but he can easily become too inbred.

But whether it be part-time or full-time the chaplain's responsibility is the same, and the pastoral opportunity is a very real one. For many people going into hospital means the introduction into a strange new world; separation from home and family; time for reflection; dependence upon other people; and often possession by hidden fears which the patient will not admit even to himself. It means being introduced suddenly, no matter how much the emphasis is on recovery and getting well, into an environment in which some people (physically) do not get better. For many who have lived sheltered and often lonely lives it entails the unexpected initiation into a community, but it is a community brought together by one need, namely that of expert medical care. A good chaplain will know of these things and will deal with people in this situation, respecting integrity and endeavouring to serve. He will try to co-operate in a total restoration to full health; he will endeavour to preserve a sense of the wholeness of the person, and see such a respect as his particular contribution. He must remember that the hospital patient is not in a position to 'avoid' his ministrations. This demands self-restraint in the chaplain and a nice awareness of the 'convenient season'.

Equally specialised, but in a different way, are chaplains to schools, to Her Majesty's Forces, to prisons and to particular institutions.

There are now in the Church of England not far short of one thousand clergy serving in the capacity of chaplains, in the main to independent schools. They are usually appointed by the headmaster and many of them meet together once a year at an annual conference. Once again these men have a specialised function, in that they are working within an institution which is a community of the young, and as such a protected community. Usually (but not always) the chaplain is in charge of the worship in the chapel. He teaches divinity and possibly one other subject; prepares boys for confirmation; and has a general pastoral oversight. A great deal, so far as his effectiveness amongst the boys is concerned, will depend upon the relationship of the chaplain to the headmaster and the rest of the staff. He needs to be able to hold his own in the common-room, not necessarily as a great intellectual but as a man of integrity and insight, committed to doing a real job of work. It is essential that he should enter into the full life of the school. He will not win the right kind of respect by courting popularity but by feeling sufficiently secure to make mature personal relations. His, indeed, is a difficult and exacting task and has become the more so in the ambiguous and challenging world of to-day, in which accepted standards of personal behaviour are exposed to agonising reappraisal, and the ruthlessly competitive demands of 'O' and 'A' levels press in upon so many young people. The chaplain will never discharge his function simply by teaching Divinity in a formal and propositional way in the classroom, or by taking advantage of the impressionability of young people, thereby winning assents which they will later resent. He needs imagination equally in the chapel as in class, so that he can redeem what happens there from becoming a merely routine operation laid on by necessary authority because this is expected.

Introducing young people into the kind of commitment for which Christian Faith stands and suggesting its implication in the spheres of life and work may well seem a daunting task to undertake, particularly in a school, and there are really no blueprints as to how it can best be done. The temptation is to confuse loyalty to the institution with loyalty to a world-wide Christian church. When this happens the religion of the chapel will be discarded once school-days are left behind. Yet loyalty to the school need not be despised but should be seen as part of a far larger whole. The chaplain needs to be himself alive as a person, excitingly experimentalist, but experimentalist against a background of firm conviction. He needs to be able to give a 'reason' for the hope that is in him, and sensitive to the scepticism which is not always out of place particularly in a young person. That there is a worth-while and unique job for him to do, there can I think be no doubt. No other kind of person could do it in quite the same way, for in addition to his own qualities as a man, for better or for worse, he is the representative of a wider Christian community.

In the environment of a school, a bad chaplain is worse than no chaplain at all, for the assessment and estimate of a whole set of ideas and values may for the boys be linked up with their assessment of him as a person. Thus if his teaching of Divinity falls below the level of the form room generally; or if the chaplain's integrity and obvious concern do not measure up to the rest of the staff, then unfortunate inferences will be drawn from this inadequacy. Such may equally be the case with any kind of community, but particularly is it so in this context, for it is often difficult for young people to separate the reality from the imperfect expression of it. The dedicated chaplain will be able to do a great deal to help individual boys if he can win their confidence, but he will do this, not by thrusting himself upon them, but by being content to be at hand when they want him.

Chaplains at colleges have in the past tended to be appointed more for academic than for pastoral ability, though it must not be assumed for a moment that there is any necessary dichotomy between the two. Recently, however, appointments have been made which were obviously determined in the main by pastoral rather than purely academic considerations. This probably represents a recognition that many young people pass through periods of great unsettlement while at college and that they certainly need help of the right kind.

The linking up of a teaching responsibility with a faith commitment, such as is entered into by a priest, can be significant when they go together in the right person. The connection between Christianity and teaching is, of course, an ancient one. Many collegiate institutions are ecclesiastical in origin, and for a very long time teaching was mainly in the hands of the clergy.

To-day a number of them are still engaged as full-time school-masters, though their deployment in state controlled schools very largely depends on the policy adopted by the local authority in consultation with the Minister of Education. It would not, perhaps, be easy to see what 'extra' is given to their instruction by the fact that they are priests, nor perhaps is this the right question to ask. Maybe even to the young, the clergyman seems to be more deeply rooted in the structure of the church, and thereby carries some other reference along with him. For this reason the ordained teacher may help to suggest that faith and intellectual integrity are not, and must never be allowed to become, incompatible. Some ordained clergy lecture or hold chairs at universities, principally in theology and related biblical or historical studies, while others teach in theological and training colleges. Such posts by no means necessarily demand ordained ministers, and it is a good thing that this responsibility should be shared by laymen. There is value, however, in having in universities ordained men of high academic and intellectual attainments, not simply that they may teach their own subject, but that they may add something to, and learn from, the life of the university in general and the senior common room in particular. Where, I suspect, it is more necessary that laymen should be in evidence is in the theological college since the training is intended in part to be practical in character. Here, alas, they are conspicuous by their absence.

Prisons and reformatory institutions generally are run by the state and the state provides that each should have an Anglican chaplain, as well as chaplains of other denominations.

Once again the responsibility of the chaplain is precisely the same as that of a priest with a pastoral responsibility anywhere —to try to lift the community which he serves, with the members who compose it, into a personal order more nearly approxima-ting to the Kingdom of God. The prison chaplain confronts particular difficulties in this specialised work, but these do not principally arise from the fact that he is dealing with an un-usually perverse society. The link between the prisoners is not that they share a common entry into sin, except in so far as this is true of any society, but that they have all indulged in patterns of anti-social behaviour, have all passed through a court of law, and as a consequence been taken from their families and deprived of their liberty. It is impossible to go through an ordeal of this kind without suffering injury as a person, and it is in this milieu that the chaplain endeavours to minister. Once again he serves the whole community, though some of its personnel will be ministered to by priests of their own communion. By the whole community I mean prison staff with their families as well as prisoners, to all of whom he is required to be a priest and invited to become a friend. In the nature of the case his is exacting work and has its own peculiar challenges and disappointments. An initial difficulty lies in the fact that the chaplain is 'laid on' by the authority which inflicts the punishment; and in the nature of the case such punishment, even if the concept of punishment is accepted as a valid one, can never be fully just in respect of the individual who receives it. The German philosopher Hegel maintained that a punishment, to be absolutely 'right', must be such that the prisoner, if he were sufficiently mature and knowledgeable, would impose it upon himself. This may be true, but it represents an ideal and very rarely an actual situation. Usually the prisoner does not see his punishment this way; and it must surely be admitted that if the *only* task of society was to reform, reformation would not begin by depriving a man of liberty, separating him from his home and family, and rendering it largely unnecessary for him to make responsible decisions. Such a deprivation is, of course, a challenge to the chaplain and makes it more important than ever that he be capable of entering into effective personal relations in spite of the unnatural conditions of prison life. Often the prisoners will wish to talk to the chaplain about their home and family, particularly since he is in a position to reassure an anxious relative.

Within the prison, the chaplain's relations with the governor and the rest of his staff are supremely important, because upon their co-operation will often depend a real opportunity of doing his job and becoming effective. Certainly there is a task waiting for him to do. A Faith that is rooted in hope, and claims to release power ought to be capable of becoming meaningful in an environment where both are desperately needed. Yet the chaplain cannot in practice detach himself in his ministry from the rightness or the wrongness of the prison system as a whole; and often, particularly in the case of the recidivist and the long-term prisoner, he will find himself working against the inexorable effects of a steady deterioration across the years. A discussion of this problem is, of course, irrelevant to the present book nor is the present writer competent to embark upon it; but the work of the chaplain must be seen within this context of the total life of the prison. He will be helped, or handicapped, by its general ethos, and in my judgment the fact that capital punishment still exists, even in a minimal form, makes his task just that bit more difficult.

Nor, as suggested earlier, is his ministry confined to the men undergoing sentence. The warders and prison staff are themselves subjected to exceptional strain and the post of the governor is one of unique authority. It is the chaplain's task to be of service to them, and he will be helped in this if he is able to see himself as the minister of a reconciling Gospel. Often the chaplain, oppressed by a sense of failure, will on his own behalf need their help and encouragement. They are all in it together.

Essentially the chaplain is where he is as a minister of the church of Christ to make whole: and he will only do this by introducing himself, as well as those around him, into resources of power. He will need to translate commitment to Jesus into immediate terms, to give it reality, not simply as an expectation for the prisoner when he gains his release, but here and now in the present. One is reminded of the remarkable testimonies of hope which emerged from some of the prisoners in the concentration camps of central Europe. The prisoner in the loneliness (though not necessarily, these days, in the solitariness) of his cell, and in the bitterness of family separation, may well give up hope or become stoically indifferent to his fate. He needs to be sustained not only by the *promise* of life but by immediate entry into it. Increasingly, and for this we may indeed be grateful, reclamation is seen as one of the chief ends of the penal system in civilised countries, though it must be admitted that, other things being equal, and they are not equal, no one who intended reformation as the sole object would plan a prison system as it at present exists. Thus it is within an environment in part resistant to what he is trying to do (for society sees itself as needing protection in the interim period before any reformation can set in) that the work of the chaplain lies.

The forces of the Crown—the Navy, the Army and the Air Force—are also state maintained and the appropriate departments of the Ministry of Defence appoint chaplains who come under the 'Chaplains' Departments'. They are members of the Service, and in the Army and the Air Force have rank and wear uniform. The function of these chaplains is precisely the same as the chaplain of any other institution, though the context within which they work is different. As in all specialised departments, there are particular difficulties inherent in the nature of the institution itself. The fact that in all the Services the chaplain is part of the establishment has its advantages and disadvantages. It means that he is accepted, taken for granted, and able to move about easily and without fuss. It also, however, means that entering into a class or hierarchal structure at a particular level (I am not referring to the Navy here) he will not always find it easy to become equally a friend to all and sundry and to make really alive personal relationships. Here the chaplain is in a different position from a commanding officer who has to fulfil another rôle; for the former must never allow his relations to become formal and confined within the rigidities of Service protocol, necessary though such protocol may be. Nor must he be asked to keep up a position other than that which is necessary to make him a valuable chaplain. He stands essentially for a personal order and must somehow break out of the structure within which he works while at the same time respecting its necessities. Perhaps it is inspired commonsense which counts here, and enables a man to do this.

In stressing the difficulty of the chaplain's position I would not for a moment wish to suggest that it constitutes an insuperable barrier to effective work which is obviously untrue: but simply that it has to be reckoned with in order that it may be overcome. Every occupation has difficulties as well as opportunities. The dedicated chaplain will accept his situation and endeavour to see that his personal relationships with officers as well as with men, are frank and uninhibited. He will realistically recognise that though he has a *quasi* independent status in that he is answerable to the Chaplains' Department, he will not in practice be able to do his job unless he is *persona grata* with the commanding officer. This does not mean, for one single moment, a sycophantic or insecure relationship: far from it; but the *nous* to understand where authority lies, and that it is within a given structure that he must build his personal order. That the chaplain can come in on this general situation in a unique way may I think, be taken for granted. Men and officers *will* come to him for help and advice if his status as a priest and his character as a man add up to a whole and rounded person. For myself I feel bound to add, though this is purely a personal view, that in the nature of the case the chaplain's work is not made easier by the problem inherent in the tension between the violence of war and the *agape* of Christian faith. The presupposition of the services must be the concept of the just war, but this is becoming increasingly more difficult to maintain convincingly in the age of the nuclear deterrent. True most of the men in the Services tend not to think in such final terms, but the chaplain cannot ignore the fact that it is within this ultimate sanction that he ministers.

The Services are still, by and large, a male establishment, with its personnel separated for long periods from their families. The chaplain needs a great deal of tact and understanding and if he is equipped with these he will be able to deal with anxieties and straighten out misunderstandings in a way which is probably easier for him than for anyone else.

Chaplains, whether in school or university, in hospital, in prison or in the Services, have one thing in common. They are provided with a community to which they minister. In this they differ from the parish priest. But basically of course the chaplain is effective only when he evokes a free response from those for whom he is necessarily responsible. Indeed the fact that his congregation *is* provided can make for resentment and build up resistances. That is why it is the overall impact of the chaplain which is important, how far he encourages relationships of trust and inspires confidence; how far in his private life he suggests the Gospel which he endeavours to mediate. Ordinary men grow tired of the back-slapping parson whose very geniality and anxiety to please are the expression of his own insecurity. Men expect the chaplain to have 'got' something and if he hasn't, it will not be long before others are aware of his lack. In this case the only thing he has to offer is his own desperate sense of need.

A remarkable indication of a need, thrown up by changed social habits, which the church can help to meet, is seen in the chaplains employed in his holiday camps by Sir Billy Butlin. It is reckoned that about 1,500,000 people per year spend their holidays in these camps; and five full-time and twenty-three part-time chaplains serve, under the Senior Chaplain, to minister to their wants. In addition to the holiday population, the camps are being used as social clubs in the winter and had a membership in 1963 of 65,000. The spiritual needs and guidance of these people are looked upon as the responsibility of the chaplains who do the work of the church in Butlin's.

Often people on holiday, away from what they see as the hum-drum life and their day-to-day environment, are willing and anxious to talk to a clergyman on the spot about their own needs and problems. It is the very anonymity of the chaplain which encourages them to talk freely. The value of such a ministry can hardly be exaggerated.

We now turn to a small number of Anglican clergy (and not only Anglicans) who are usually styled industrial chaplains. These priests live their lives within industry either themselves exercising a pastoral responsibility or advising the bishop and clergy in the diocese on matters relating to the church and an industrial society. The fact that such chaplains should exist is the frank recognition that the parish priest in particular, and the church in general, find it difficult to make any effective contact with the industrial worker, a situation which goes right back to the age of the Industrial Revolution. One often hears the statement that the church has lost its hold on the factory worker. If this is meant to imply that there was a time when it had such a hold the assumption is a false one.

The emergence of the industrial chaplain is also testimony to the solidarity of the class structures and the strength of the group interests which involvement together in an industrial enterprise brings with it. This was one of the great themes implied in Karl Marx's *Das Kapital*, and at the psychological level there is undoubtedly a great deal of truth in it. It is the industrial chaplain's concern to get inside the skin of the man in the factory and to be available to all, worker and director alike. He is not there to usurp the function of the welfare officer nor of the local minister, but to deal with workers and directors as members of a personal order, though this personal order is conditioned, and consequently the relationships within it, by the exigencies of economic production. His task cannot be easy, particularly as it is likely to be misunderstood by both management and men. Only an exceptional person can hope to introduce himself into such a set-up and be effective. He needs a special training which enables him to think theologically within a secular context. He needs to be rooted in this structure and alive to its more than industrial relevance. Little is done at the moment to produce such men in the theological colleges; and it is pioneers, such as Ted Wickham, now Bishop of Middleton, who have largely inspired and produced such people. Good-will of itself may help but it is not enough, nor will a hearty camaraderie prove a substitute for intelligence, knowledge, and an adult concern. There is certainly room here for much more thought and experiment. Relations within a modern factory are themselves so complex that it is not easy to see precisely where the industrial chaplain comes into it. The rigid distinction between skilled and unskilled labour, the too frequent tension between the steward on the shop floor and trade union official (the latter smacking of the black coated worker), the cleavage between management and employee, do not help the industrial chaplain who, if he seems to be on one side rather than the other, immediately invites a suspicion which shades off into open hostility. The fact is that if men are to be helped by the chaplain in the factory, they cannot be withdrawn from their total situation and therefore the interplay of interests and the collision of classes cannot be ignored.

This general situation is not, of course, unique to the English scene. The Roman Catholic Church in Italy is deeply exercised at the growing inroads of communism in that country, not only in the poverty-stricken areas in the south (where it might be expected) but in the more affluent and industrial areas of the north.

The ambiguous and uncertain status of the industrial chaplain has prompted some ordained ministers of the Church of England to become workers themselves. I am reminded in this context of a short story, I think by D. H. Lawrence, in which he depicts a miner from the north of England after shipwreck in the Channel being taken, after rescue, into the home of a French mining family. He cannot speak a word of the language, but he is immediately at home. Their life, like his, is regulated around the ruthless demands of the pit. They bath in the same way in the kitchen (the story is some fifty years old!) and he is at his ease, so powerful are occupation and environment in moulding human sympathy and understanding.

The worker-priests, I use this description for the want of a better term, do not constitute a closely knit community nor would they claim to have a clear cut *rationale* of their particular function. They witness in faith. They do not in the factory exercise their orders and some of them are not necessarily known to be 'ministers of religion'. What they do is simply to enter into the day-to-day life of the factory as workers, often as unskilled. They become shop-stewards if they are elected; and they share completely in their homes the economic pattern of family living characteristic of the industrial workers around them. In exceptional cases the worker-priest may be attached to a parish church but this is not usual. In so far as he may be said to have a guiding inspiration it is to be found in the Franciscan ideal of identity and compassion. Such a ministry is sacrificial and self-giving, leading to a real and not formal identity. It is the demand, so the worker-priest believes, which love and caring make upon him. As one of their number has written: 'We are trying to represent a fashion of life demanded by the Gospel . . .

K

the fashion which rejects wealth and worldly power . . . until *all* are able to hold wealth and power and all have become free citizens of the Kingdom of God.'

As I have suggested, most of such men do not see the way ahead of them at all clearly, but they are convinced that the factory floor is the place where they, as priests, ought to be and that through their presence the church is rooted in the industrial order in a unique way. This is incarnation.

It is not for me to make any assessment of the respective merits of the industrial chaplain and the worker-priest, the one who goes into the factory as a chaplain, introducing himself on to the floor and into the board room, and the other who becomes involved as a fully committed worker with no strings attached, associating his family in the same process of identity.

Maybe the industrial chaplain will prove effective in so far as he can be sensitive to the sectional interests with which he comes into contact, while at the same time transcending them all. A prerequisite is a man of strong and independent character, who is known to be such and whose integrity is beyond question. In factories where the cleavage between management and men is deep-seated—and this is more likely to be the case in certain classes of industrial production—his task will be made the more difficult. Industrial chaplains, however, represent a creative development which should become more normative in the future.

The worker-priest does not meet this particular kind of difficulty, since it is his vocation to engage himself in industry at a particular level and at this level to become part of it. He does not seek to transcend the class structure, and in this sense his task is less complicated, though he has of course his own particular problems.

It must not be forgotten that the parish priest will try to make some kind of contact with the factories within his parish, and he has one advantage in that this is a perfectly natural thing for him to do as part of his normal ministry. Also he has the opportunity of meeting the industrial worker in his home—where he is just a person.

Most bishops appoint youth chaplains who advise generally

on the church's work among young people, and are active in co-ordinating what is going on in the parish and inspiring to fresh activity. They also make contact with the local authority.

At this point, it is necessary to refer to one class of priests who differ in many respects from those mentioned earlier. I refer to the religious orders.

The religious orders, as such, were suppressed in England at the time of the Reformation, and for a very long period afterwards there was a strong prejudice against them as both Roman and superstitious. They were revived in the nineteenth century under the impetus of the Oxford Movement, and it is now true that the great historic orders, the Benedictines and the Franciscans, exist within the Church of England. The various communities differ amongst themselves in accordance with their rule and the traditions which they have inherited. Some are actively social within the context of a rhythm of worship. Others are in general more contemplative in character and see their main vocation in terms of an objective offering of prayer and worship. That the revival of these communities has added enormously to the vitality and richness of the Church of England there can be no doubt. This is not surprising since the contribution of such orders to the shaping of western Europe has in the past been tremendous. They helped to pilot the civilisation of Rome into the new Europe which emerged after the break-up of the Empire. Later they made possible the splendid achievements of the Middle Ages, adding to its scholarship, its missionary enterprise, even its farming. Though the 'double standard' which gave priority to a life vowed to poverty, chastity and obedience can no longer command our assent, yet the abandonment of an older apologia has by no means taken away the significance or relevance in a contemporary situation of the religious orders. Their cultivation of the interior life, their concentration upon community, their social and missionary zeal, their scholarship, indeed their manoeuvrability—all these give added impetus and strength to the church, which would be far poorer without this particular witness.

Mention must now be made of the many clergy who are neither chaplains, teachers, industrial chaplains, worker-priests nor members of religious orders. I shall refer to them briefly, though this must not be taken to mean that their work is unimportant.

Perhaps, first of all, there should be mentioned the great missionary societies, such as the Society for Propagating the Gospel and the Church Missionary Society, which have on their staff (as well, of course, as devoted priests actively engaged in the field all over the world) clergymen in administrative and secretarial posts. The importance of their work in planning a literally world-wide strategy, and linking up the distant missionary with his home base can hardly be exaggerated. These men are in key positions, at a time when there is a new confrontation of the ancient Faiths of East and West, and when history may well be on the march once more.

Also many societies, engaged in good works, employ travelling and appeal secretaries who are Church of England clergymen— for example, the National Society, the Missions to Seamen, the Church of England's Children's Society, the United Society for Christian Literature and many others. Indeed the list is a long one. The reasons for such appointments are threefold. First, as clergy, they can preach in Anglican pulpits. Secondly they have often had experience in the field of work that the Society seeks to commend. Thirdly they can usually be employed more cheaply than laymen. Whether these are a sufficient justification for their deployment in this way may be questioned, but I do not myself believe in being too doctrinaire in matters of this kind. There is something to be said for spreading the clergy around and seeing that amongst them are those who have a particular experience in specialised walks of life. Often a man who has grown stale in parochial work can well benefit for a period from a different experience. As suggested earlier, the presence of a priest (rightly or wrongly) is seen as denoting the presence of the church in a unique way. He is a representative person, even if a few priests are just themselves, with their own unique flair and range of interests.

I now turn, finally, to a group of clergy who in our contemporary world are in a position to exercise an enormous influence over vast masses of people. I refer to the Anglican clergy who (with clergy of other denominations) are responsible for religious broadcasting on both sound and television. It is almost impossible to exaggerate the importance of their work, particularly in the effect which it has in suggesting the image of Christianity to modern (often) unchurched and secular men. Their task is not easy for the problems inherent in any form of mass (indiscriminate) communication are immense and have not yet been solved. In my own judgment those who discharge this responsibility have succeeded in making religious broadcasting significant; they have given it a cutting edge, and rescued it from the pedestrian and the commonplace, which it could all too easily have become. These Anglican clergy, it is important to add, are appointed and employed by the bodies which they serve, whether it be the British Broadcasting Corporation or the appropriate authority in Independent Television.

POSTSCRIPT

THIS book has, in the main, been concerned with the parish priest, and rightly, because he constitutes by far the majority of working Anglican clergymen. Since the days when the illiterate Anglo-Saxon priest, maintained by the local lord, first witnessed to the Christian Gospel, the parish priest has endeavoured to build the Kingdom of Christ sometimes with, sometimes without, zeal. The social scene has changed and the political structure of the nation undergone a vast transformation. The Church of England severed its link with Rome. Its clergy were dispossessed during the middle of the seventeenth century, at ease for the most part during the eighteenth, and passed through a period of comparative opulence in the nineteenth century.

Yet the security of the nineteenth-century scene in which the parish priest introduced himself, almost snugly, into the class structure of Victorian England seems more remote to-day than does the Rome of Cicero. Its outward symbols may still be with us in the National School, the spacious rectory and lawn, the photographs of the surpliced choir hanging in the vestry, and the restored church. Yet the substance behind them has vanished. Indeed it seems impossible, as we contemplate these visible signs, to realise that they were realities so recently.

The modern parish priest finds himself in a different world and one in which so much more seems to depend on him personally. It is not surprising that he anxiously asks himself, from time to time, how precisely he fits into it. The integrity of the village is no more; populations are on the whole mobile; commuting is the new pattern; and the densely populated parishes of industrial subtopia or the middle-class suburban areas mean that in practice all he can hope to do personally is to touch a small fringe of the population. To large numbers of his people the church and what happens within it seem simply irrelevant. It is not so much that modern technological man is caught up in a violent secularism or anti-clericalism but that all too often he does not see the church as sufficiently significant to be worth opposing. The intellectual climate is not, perhaps, so favourable to Christian Faith as optimists too often suppose.

The Anglican clergyman in the parish has lost much (but not all) of his privileged status—by which I mean the status that he held for a short time a century ago.* Education, which often began in a church school, is now taken out of his hands. Social services laid on by the welfare state have ceased to owe very much to a direct Christian initiative; recreation, which the church often inspired, no longer needs its paternal care.

In other words the parish priest of to-day is stripped of many of the accretions of power and influence which in a particular historical situation grew up around his predecessors. With so many responsibilities removed from him, and his stature seemingly and correspondingly reduced, is there any longer a place for him? Are not other people now doing on a wider scale what he in an amateur way, even if in a pioneer capacity, tried to initiate?

The answer to the latter of the two questions must be 'Yes', but to the first and more fundamental, it is in my judgment a most emphatic 'No', as this book has tried to suggest.

Indeed the very severity of the contemporary challenge, and the seeming deprivations from which the parish priest suffers, may be the means of his rediscovering himself and his true vocation in a new situation. Social patterns are never static, and the priest must incarnate himself anew in ever changing scenes. The accretions are not of the essence of his office, though they may well have been essential to its expression at a particular time. Though a naïve optimism must at all costs be avoided, it is equally important to remember that the personal order for which the priest finally stands is as relevant to-day as it has ever been. To proclaim it becomes even more necessary in an age which is tempted to close the order of parsons as the Renaissance did the order of nature. Of course, to establish a personal order in an industrial and technological society presents its own

* The eighteenth-century clergyman was certainly not in this position.

problems, but this I suspect makes the priest's contribution even more significant, relevant, and necessary. He will be enabled to make it only if he is prepared to involve himself and work from within. He still leads or is integral to the worship of the community which meets in the parish church and which in its very nature is part of a world-wide community transcending race and colour. He still intervenes in the lives of many people at their most significant moments. He still has a measure of good-will to come in upon as he visits in his parish. He is still in a position to see a person steadily and to see him whole, to glimpse beyond the worker into the home from which he sets out and to which he and his family return. He still mediates a Faith which, if it ever was true, is still true; and he communicates it to men often faintly insecure within themselves, who desperately need both vision and power.

Certainly to exercise his priesthood in the modern world, when society is far more fluid and less patterned than it has been for a long time, asks more of him as a person. He has little social prestige in his own right to fall back upon. Yet in a world of increasing scientific application, when power of necessity must be placed in fewer hands, he may expect to find a great and increasing hunger for the order for which he stands. The parish priest believes that this personal order is rooted in the eternity of God and that Jesus showed the way and releases the power by which we can move towards it.

Yes! there is a great task waiting to be done by the parish priest; but he will be stretched to the utmost in the doing of it and he will most certainly find it a tough assignment.

'Who is sufficient for these things?'

INDEX